BEHIND THE BAR

Stories from a Pastorista

SHANNON GREER

WestBow Press
A DIVISION OF THOMAS NELSON
& ZONDERVAN

Copyright © 2022 Shannon Greer.

All rights reserved. No part of this book may be used or reproduced by any means, graphic, electronic, or mechanical, including photocopying, recording, taping or by any information storage retrieval system without the written permission of the author except in the case of brief quotations embodied in critical articles and reviews.

This book is a work of non-fiction. Unless otherwise noted, the author and the publisher make no explicit guarantees as to the accuracy of the information contained in this book and in some cases, names of people and places have been altered to protect their privacy.

WestBow Press books may be ordered through booksellers or by contacting:

WestBow Press
A Division of Thomas Nelson & Zondervan
1663 Liberty Drive
Bloomington, IN 47403
www.westbowpress.com
844-714-3454

Because of the dynamic nature of the Internet, any web addresses or links contained in this book may have changed since publication and may no longer be valid. The views expressed in this work are solely those of the author and do not necessarily reflect the views of the publisher, and the publisher hereby disclaims any responsibility for them.

Any people depicted in stock imagery provided by Getty Images are models, and such images are being used for illustrative purposes only. Certain stock imagery © Getty Images.

Scripture quotations marked CSB have been taken from the Christian Standard Bible®, Copyright © 2017 by Holman Bible Publishers. Used by permission. Christian Standard Bible® and CSB® are federally registered trademarks of Holman Bible Publishers.

ISBN: 978-1-6642-5376-6 (sc)
ISBN: 978-1-6642-5377-3 (hc)
ISBN: 978-1-6642-5375-9 (e)

Library of Congress Control Number: 2021925461

Print information available on the last page.

WestBow Press rev. date: 02/17/2022

— MY TRIBE —

Kristia, Makenzie, Madilynn, Josie, Jayden & Arielle.

CONTENTS

Introduction ix

Chapter 1	More 1
Chapter 2	Seen and Not Heard 5
Chapter 3	Disguise 12
Chapter 4	What If 17
Chapter 5	Cadence 24
Chapter 6	Church in Reverse 28
Chapter 7	No Accidents 34
Chapter 8	Real People 40
Chapter 9	Normal 46
Chapter 10	Lower the Bar 52
Chapter 11	Epic 58
Chapter 12	Miracles 64
Chapter 13	Band-Aids 70
Chapter 14	Outlaw 76
Chapter 15	Lifeline 81
Chapter 16	Table in the Corner 88
Chapter 17	Unknown 94
Chapter 18	Jesus Stuff 101
Chapter 19	Help Wanted 107
Chapter 20	Get It 113

Chapter 21	Hard Day	119
Chapter 22	Ordinary	125
Chapter 23	Family Affair	133
Chapter 24	Lean	138
Chapter 25	Real Jesus	144

Epilogue 151

INTRODUCTION

Have you ever stopped to consider what life would look like for Jesus if He was visibly living here on the earth today? Where would He live? How would He spend His time? Where would He spend most of that time and with whom?

If you had asked me those questions years ago, I would have given you the typical Christian answers because I would expect Him to be in Christian places, living among Christian people. In fact, that's where and how I figured I was supposed to live my life—surrounded by all things Christian.

I grew up in a Christian home. Mom and Dad made sure our family was in church every time the doors were opened. Christian music was what we listened to in the car, and although I went to a public or secular school, I did grow up in a Christian town. OK, so Christiansburg, Virginia, wasn't exactly a Christian town, but it sounded Christian.

After I graduated from high school, I went to a Christian college, and while there were plenty of sinners on campus, it was still a very Christian environment. We had chapel three times each week, and one week out of every semester, we had a convocation, which was a solid week of two chapel services each day. Most professors started their classes with a devotion or prayer time. The college was even marketed as "The Campus Where Christ Is King." I remember leaving that campus for a weekend and feeling like I was getting dirty being out in the world.

When I graduated from college, I felt called to full-time vocational ministry—working for a Christian organization. I served as a missionary, and while living in a foreign country, I gravitated to and spent much of my day-to-day living among Christians. When my wife and I returned to the States, I applied for various youth and associate pastor jobs around the country. When none of those positions panned out, we decided to plant our own church. Surely that's what Jesus would do—plant a new church. I worked for a year in a secular job, but I felt so out of place, like a fish out of water. This was not where I belonged; I was convinced that God wanted me to be in a Christian environment. That, and the church plant idea was a bust. So, I left the secular job, left the whole idea of the church plant behind, and transitioned into full-time vocational ministry again, working at a ministry headquarters. My coworkers were all Christians. We had devotions and prayer times together. We played worship music all day, every day. It was heaven on earth. I knew that if Jesus were living my life in the late nineties and early 2000s, He would definitely be where I was spending my time and energy.

A few years later, I went on staff at a growing church in south Alabama. What says *Christian job* like a church job? My days were filled with meetings with other pastors and church volunteers. I had arrived in a Christian dream world. This was most definitely the place you would find Jesus if He were physically living here on earth.

One day as I drove home from another day of full-time ministry, I began to realize that I had only Christian friends. Not one person in my circle of friends was an outsider to the Christian faith. I knew a few Christians who acted like sinners, but I didn't have a single sinner friend.

That thought was the catalyst that caused me to reevaluate my whole life, what I felt called to do. I began reevaluating where I spent my time and with whom I spent that time. Now I wasn't blazing trails to bars, clubs, or other dens of iniquity. But I did begin to seriously ask some life-changing questions.

Where would Jesus *go*?
What would Jesus *do*?
Where would Jesus *work*?
With *whom* would Jesus have coffee?

Those questions led me down a path that I've been traveling for more than ten years now. They led me behind the bar of a coffee shop where I began engaging with people who were not like me at all. I started caring for them. I had meaningful conversations with them. I began living life with people who were not part of my Christian tribe. As a result, my purpose and my calling began to change. Maybe it didn't really change; maybe I changed, or maybe things just became clearer as to how and where and with whom I was to live my life.

All my life, I saw myself becoming a pastor. As a small child, my parents and family members would ask me what I hoped to be when I grew up.

On cue, without blinking an eye, I would square my shoulders back, look them dead in the eye, and declare, "I'm going to be a preacher, and I'm going to preach about the Father, the Son, and the Holy Ghost."

I'd get a smile, a laugh, and a pat on the head with a "That's cute" or "Precious." I suppose it was on some level.

But as an adult, something was shifting. I found myself a barista and a pastor, two unlikely career paths to ever merge. But God was blending those two roles. I wasn't just a pastor, and I wasn't just a barista. He was shaping me into "pastorista." Now He never officially called me that. There was no James Earl Jones voice that ever said, "From this day and every day henceforth, thou shalt be called pastorista." I made up the name, but He created the calling. This was who He intended me to be.

What has happened in my life since has been a daily discovery of Jesus—learning with whom He would live life and learning to love them like He would if He were physically living here on earth.

I could tell you story after story of how I've seen Jesus behind the bar of an inconspicuous little coffee shop in downtown Chattanooga. In fact, that's why you are holding this book in your hands. Because I want you to see Jesus in the places and with the people that I've seen Him. My hope is that after you read these stories, you, too, will begin to look for Him in places other than the usual Christian places you might expect. I hope that you will see Jesus leading you to cross paths with people who aren't like you and that those people will see Jesus, too, not necessarily in the church building but on display in your life.

So, grab a cup of coffee, and let me take you behind the bar to show you where and how I've seen Jesus.

1

MORE

I was nervous. I had been on plenty of interviews in my lifetime, but this was a bit of a stretch for me. I had never worked in a coffee shop before. I certainly had wanted to. Before this job, I sold life insurance. Well, I did for a week. I took home $1.57 in my first and last paycheck. Yeah, you read that right. My family had moved to Chattanooga to plant a church in June of that year. It was August, and I needed a job—desperately.

One night while we were gathered with our launch team, a friend mentioned that the company where she worked owned a coffee shop, and it was looking to fill a position. I was interested. I went the next day to fill out an application.

A year before, I had considered applying for Starbucks when we lived in Alabama. I was on staff as an associate senior pastor and had a full job description at a church that was a stone's throw from Starbucks. Multiple times each week, I would go there and have meetings with Trey, my best friend and colleague.

One morning while we were having coffee, I overheard the barista greeting customers as they came in. "Hey, Jim, are you getting your usual today?"

"Yes, ma'am."

"How was your son's soccer game last night? Did they win?"

"They did! They played hard, and they won."

The conversation went on. The barista knew so much more about Jim than the kind of coffee he ordered every day. That affected me. So much of my day-to-day was spent in one meeting after another, talking about small groups, church programs, budgets, and ways to grow the church. That was OK, but man, I would love to be behind that bar getting to know people, hearing their stories, and making them part of mine.

I took an application and filled it out, but how would it look for an associate senior pastor of a growing megachurch to be working behind the bar at Starbucks? What would people think? I chickened out and never turned that application in.

This time, though, I didn't need a second job. I needed a job—one that paid more than $1.57. I sat there at the table in the front window of the quaint café on Market Street. My wife, Kristia, enjoyed a blended hot chocolate while I frantically wrote down references and corresponding telephone numbers. I turned the application in to the cashier, and within the next twenty-four hours, I answered a call from Eric, the manager. He was professional, friendly, and eager to meet, so the next day, I met him at two o'clock for my interview.

My palms were sweaty, and my deodorant was working overtime. I didn't know the difference between a mocha or a latte. All I knew about coffee was that I liked it.

If my hope of landing this job hinged on my knowledge of coffee, I was doomed from the start.

We sat outside at the green bistro table in front of the café. The smell was amazing. Regular customers walked in and out of the front door. Each one greeted Eric like an old friend. He tried to stay present and focused on the interview, but his customer-service skills compelled him to greet every customer as they entered, at least with a cordial nod and smile.

We went through the formalities.

"Tell me about your family. What brings you to Chattanooga?"

That's about as far as we made it into the actual interview. He seemed to be intrigued that this thirtysomething-year-old dad of three was applying for what would essentially be a busboy position. They fancied it up and called it a "back bar" position, but if I got the job, I would be a busboy. I would make sure condiment counters were restocked and shuttles of coffee were brewed and ready to serve during the morning rushes. I didn't care what the job entailed; I was willing and ready, silently praying that God would make this guy like me and offer me the job. I needed the job.

He was intrigued by the fact that our family had moved to Chattanooga to plant a church, and the reasons why. Chattanooga was home to more than one thousand churches, and the last thing this enclave of the Bible Belt needed was another church. He was pushing the buttons, though, hitting those conversation points that I loved to talk about. So that's what we talked about. The next thing I knew, he looked at his watch and seemed surprised that we had been talking for an hour. He had to run to his next appointment. He stood up, shook my hand, thanked me for coming, and told me he would call me to let me know what he had decided.

I walked to my car feeling conflicted. I was excited about that conversation, but I didn't feel hopeful that I would get the job. All this guy wanted to talk about was the church and the church at large and his frustrations with it, and ... suddenly, I felt this cool wind blow against the back of my neck. It was a hot Thursday in August in Chattanooga, so a cool breeze was the last thing I expected to feel. It sent chills down my neck and the back of my arms. Then I felt what seemed to be like the quietest whisper in in the deepest part of my soul.

"There's more."

I froze. My finger was on the unlock button of my key fob, but I didn't push the button. I just stood there. I took in the sights around me. City buses were speeding by. The fountain at Miller Park was blasting water streams in the sky. I could hear the creaking of the heavy doors to the post office behind me as people were going in and out. So much movement around me, and there I stood frozen.

I felt Jesus. Felt Him right there beside me. Telling me that there was more going on than what I could understand or see at that moment. I felt this strong sense that He just wanted me to trust Him. More importantly, I felt like He wanted me to pay attention. He wanted me to just be aware that something significant was unfolding around me and to look for Him as He worked out the details of my life in that season. This was more than just a job interview and more than just a conversation about what was right or wrong with the local church or the church at large.

In full disclosure, I thought Eric and his family might show up one Sunday at our newly planted church. Maybe the past hour was really for him and me to meet and nothing more. Eric and his family did come to RiverChurch a few years later, but there was more happening in this moment. I didn't know it then, but that day was a red-letter day—the day when I would begin to discover the more that God had in store for me and when I would begin to discover Jesus like never before.

2

Seen and Not Heard

Before I was officially hired as the back bar at that coffee shop, I had to complete a second interview, this time with one of the owners. Eric phoned me later in the day after my interview with him and asked if I could come back the following Tuesday to meet Evelyn. Tuesday was four days away, and I was feeling impatient, but I wanted the job, so I happily agreed.

This seemed like a really big deal for what seemed to be a rather insignificant busboy role. During my first interview, Eric hadn't talked a lot about my potential responsibilities as the back bar, but he did say enough for me to know I wouldn't be driving a company car, signing company checks, or doing press releases. But if another interview was necessary, I would certainly oblige.

I arrived early. Eric met me at the door and offered me a cup of coffee. I was too nervous to drink anything. My natural inclination toward clumsiness would guarantee that I would royally ruin this one chance to make a good first impression, so I politely turned down his offer. He directed me to one of two pub tables that sat directly across from the bar.

"Evelyn will be right down."

I appreciated the time to simply sit and take in the sights and sounds of the café.

The floors were clean. Some of the small, white, octagonal tiles were chipped or marked with character blemishes, but cleanliness was obviously a big deal here.

The coffee bar and the area behind it were quaint. I've never been to a coffee shop in Paris, but this café was exactly what I imagined a coffee shop in Paris would look like.

Along the back wall were copper bins filled with freshly roasted coffee beans. Below those bins stood a large, copper coffee grinder. As I sat there, a barista stepped over to the grinder and with the push of a button made it sing. The sound of beans being crushed at rapid speed eventually transitioned to a gentle hum, indicating that every bean had been perfectly ground. And the smell—oh the smell of freshly ground coffee—filled the room, letting the whole room know that a fresh cup of goodness was moments away.

The baristas looked classy with black shirts, black pants, black shoes, black aprons, and button name tags on the top edge of each apron. The LaMarzoco espresso machine sat on the bar like a crown on a king's head. A coffee drink in a round orange mug, complete with what appeared to be a fleur-de-lis made of milk, sat on the copper-covered counter to the right of the barista, waiting to be collected by the rightful owner. The pastry case had a modest presentation of cookies, muffins, and lemon chess bars. The walls were lined with shelves of merchandise, syrup bottles, and all things coffee.

The seating area was perfectly situated with two-seater tables for customers to meet or enjoy a cup with a friend for a few minutes but not too long, since the seats weren't all that comfortable. The café was situated in the heart of the business district in Chattanooga, and the clientele was mostly folks with a finite resource of time who couldn't afford to come and sit for hours.

I took it all in, and with every second I waited for Evelyn to arrive, I was falling in love with this place. This environment, the sights, the sounds, the smells, all of it seemed to envelop me, and I wanted to work there. I whispered a quick prayer, "God, please let this interview go well."

Just then, the back door to the café opened with a click and a squeak, and a woman with snowy white hair stepped inside. She was formidable. Not pretentious but extremely professional.

"Shannon?" she asked with a quiet and peaceful presence as she shook my hand firmly.

"Hi. Yes, I'm Shannon. Evelyn?"

"Yes, have a seat."

My second interview was much shorter than my initial interview with Eric. Evelyn clearly and concisely laid out her expectations. She was cordial. My slight nervous chuckle here or there didn't seem to faze her as she told me about this café and exactly what would be expected of me as a back bar if I was hired. As she described the role, the next thing she said chaffed me.

"Basically, your job would be to be seen and not heard."

My mind seemed to lock in on those words, and my heart seemed to sink.

Wait, what? I thought.

Seen and not heard. I knew I was applying for an insignificant role, but something about that phrase felt offensive. Telling an extrovert to be seen and not heard is like telling a singer to speak softly, or a drummer to quietly tap their toes. It goes against every fiber of who we are, how we are made.

I thought working at a coffee shop meant I would get to meet lots of exciting new people, talk to them, hear their stories, tell them mine, and share some anecdotal life lessons with one another. Who knows? Maybe this would be the place I would gather new church members to my fledgling little church plant. But this … this was a hard pill to swallow—seen and not heard. What did that mean anyway? I had to stop being offended long enough to consider what Evelyn was saying.

Being seen and not heard meant being present, in the room, observing anything and everything that needed to be done and doing it without being conspicuous or interfering with a customer's experience. I was to be the quiet presence, a man in black, simply there to serve—nothing more. I could do it; I mean, I guess I could. Honestly, it sounded boring. More honestly, a little beneath me. Still, I needed the job, so I nodded my head to indicate I understood what was expected, and within a few minutes, the interview was over.

Later that evening, Eric called to offer me the job. He was excited. I was initially, but the reality of the insignificance of my role was settling in, and I wondered if I would last. I accepted and later that week began my orientation. I hit it off well with the staff—Bailey, Chase, Jeffrey, Josh, and of course Eric the manager. Besides him, I was the oldest employee at the café. I eventually met Eileen, the other owner of the company; she had oversight of other ventures of the business. We got along well when she came by, but most of my interaction with the owners was with Evelyn, and that interaction was sparse and at times uncomfortable.

Evelyn would walk into the café, and we would exchange pleasantries. It seemed that if there were things that I needed to correct or improve upon, she would communicate those things to Eric and expect him to communicate with me. She rarely gave me any direction or instruction.

Truthfully, I felt like she didn't like me. That whole "seen and not heard" bit from my interview kept rolling around in my head, and I built a narrative in my mind that she knew I was a pastor, and she was afraid I might get too churchy or something like that, so she told me that whole thing just to keep me from proselytizing customers. I played that narrative over and over in my head, to the point that I dreaded interactions with her. I avoided talking to her, even making eye contact with her. One day, she noticed.

It was around October of that year, two months after I started as back bar, that she asked to meet with me. This was it. I knew it. I was in for it.

To my surprise, she began the meeting by telling me how pleased she was with my performance over the past two months.

"I can tell that you take your job seriously, and I wanted to see if you would have any interest in moving up to the cashier spot."

"Really?" I asked in amazement. She wanted me to engage with customers.

She seemed surprised at my response and pressed in to ask why I seemed so surprised.

"It's just … you mean you want me to be a cashier? You're OK if I talk to customers?"

"Of course." She chuckled. "Why wouldn't I be?"

I proceeded to tell her how I had wrestled with the "seen and not heard" concept and how I was afraid she thought I was going to try to Billy Graham the customers when they came in. She laughed even more. "Not at all. That's just how we've structured that role as back bar."

She went on to explain that the back bar was a learning role, a place for a new employee to observe and learn while still performing important tasks. She assured me that it had nothing to do with me.

But it did. It had everything to do with me. I needed to be confronted with a reality that I had never noticed before. I discovered that I had the need to be noticed, to be seen and heard. As a Christian, I had an obligation to make it known loud and clear that I was a Bible-quoting, sin-hating, fire of God–breathing believer in Jesus. If you didn't know that after being around me for five minutes, then I was obviously failing in my role as a Christian. It was my job as a Christian to be seen *and* heard. But while Evelyn wasn't using the term to challenge me directly, I realized that God was. He was challenging my thinking and my understanding of what it meant to be a true follower of Jesus. That, and He was teaching me a good old-fashioned lesson in humility.

In those two months of being seen and not heard, I learned that I didn't have to be the center of attention, the most important person in the room. I learned the value of listening more and talking less. I learned the importance of staying in my lane, doing my part to help the entire team be successful in serving customers well. I learned that people don't always need to hear what I say nearly as much as they may need me to hear what they say. I learned that being seen and not heard is a good thing, a healthy thing. It provides a space to simply serve, to be secondary, to help.

That simple concept impacted me. Changed me. Now don't get me wrong. I still love to talk, and I have a lot to say, and sometimes I'm convinced that there are more people who need to hear what I have to say than there are people who really do. Still, I often remind myself to take a breather, to step back and observe, to listen, to be present but not noisy. It's in that position that I am best able to see the big picture, the purpose for which I was created, and the ideal opportunities to help and serve others.

Reflecting on the life and ministry of Jesus, He wasn't always the center of attention. Granted, He drew crowds who wanted to see Him do miracles. But you never read that Jesus ever grandstanded or tried to be the most important person in the room. He set an example when He washed the disciples' feet, when He slipped away from the crowds, and when he drew stick figures in the sand while religious folks were trying to get him to condemn an immoral woman. Jesus was never flashy or obtrusive. He was inconspicuous and impacting all at the same time.

Today, Jesus is rarely seen, and He's not often heard. I think that's partly because the folks who represent Him don't always do the best of jobs at that. That's another sermon for another day.

Evelyn became a dear friend. Since that first interview, she and I have shared many more conversations and many cups of coffee. She has encouraged me, challenged me, even confided in me. I sit here today at a table in front of my own coffee shop, writing this story, because of the lessons I learned under her mentorship.

Thanks, Evelyn.

3

Disguise

I picked things up quickly behind the bar. I loved being the cashier. It was definitely my sweet spot. I would be the first to greet customers as they stepped up to place their order. I was terrible at remembering names. Many of them were easier to remember by the drink they ordered. When I was away from the coffee shop, I would see regular customers out in public, and Kristia or the kids would ask, "Who is that?"

"Oh, that's Large Nonfat Sugar-Free Amaretto Latte," or

"That's Dry Cappuccino with Extra Foam."

One of the first names I remembered was Nick. At least that's what he gave me. Nick was Caucasian with obvious Native American ancestry, and he wasn't very happy with his results from 23andMe that told him he hailed from a British bloodline. Nick used to be a body builder, a real stud in his day. When I first met him, he was still pretty built, a decent-looking guy who had experienced some real rough patches in his life. He never knew his dad. He was a survivor of eighteen major car accidents, a badge he wore proudly.

One day, Nick walked into the shop wearing sunglasses, a ball cap turned around backward, long (like past the knee), extremely baggy denim shorts, an oversized T-shirt, and a thick gold chain around his neck. Conspicuous was an understatement. He was nothing at all like the typical white-collar, middle-aged businessman who frequented the café. A far cry as well from the typical mountain lady who would come downtown from Signal or Lookout Mountain for her morning yoga class and then drop in for her skinny vanilla latte, no whip.

But this day, Nick looked like he had stepped off the set of the *Fresh Prince of Bel Air*. He looked a bit uncomfortable in his own skin. Something about him seemed off. He seemed fidgety, like he was up to something, good or bad I couldn't tell. He didn't order, just waited—for Gary.

Gary was another regular who happened to walk in a few minutes after Nick. Seemingly oblivious to the oddly acting character sitting at the pub table across from the bar, Gary stepped up to the counter to order his usual double shot of espresso with a little brewed coffee added to it in an eight-ounce cup. As Gary pulled his wallet out to pay, the forty-something gangster stepped up behind him and whispered, "Give me all your money."

Gary looked at me, fully aware of my shock and uncertainty as to what was happening, and simply said in an unfazed tone of voice, "He's a clown."

Immediately, the guy behind Gary burst into laughter and took off the hat and sunglasses. I hadn't known the stranger was Nick; he had certainly fooled me. I hadn't had that many conversations with him up to that point. He thought he was hilarious, Gary thought, well ... that Nick was a clown.

These two were like salt and pepper. The closest of friends and polar opposites. Gary was a general contractor. He would often come in talking on his phone with subcontractors or customers giving or taking orders. Nick was a jack-of-all-trades. He handed me a business card one time that listed all the services he provided. It was impressive.

Yard Work
Hauling
House-Sitting
Dog Walking
Dead Animal Removal
Bounty Hunter

That last one was the reason for his gangster getup. He was on his way to pick up a guy who had skipped bail, and Nick wanted to test out his disguise on his best friend. If he could fool Gary, he knew his plan would succeed. He fooled me, not Gary, but he certainly had me.

Gary and Nick would come in every day, and watching them interact was like watching a sitcom. Nick was in fact the clown. Gary was the serious one. Still, the two of them would laugh and cut up together and obnoxiously flirt with the ladies who came in to order coffee. On more than one occasion, I had to tell them to chill out, put their eyes back in their heads, and be respectful.

"Guys, that's someone's daughter that you are ogling!"

Nothing made the blood of this dad of three girls boil like the two of them when they got to acting like a couple of middle school boys.

At least once a week, Nick would come in with a five-year-old little boy named Christopher. Nick would buy Christopher a bagel and juice. There was no family connection at all between Christopher and Nick. When Christopher was a baby, Nick picked up his mom for skipping bail. He developed some sort of relationship with her, and on one occasion when Nick had to go bring her in, she asked him to keep an eye on her baby boy. She didn't want him going to the state, so Nick agreed. He was clueless about what to do with a baby, but he took care of him and stayed in Christopher's life. When mom needed a break, Nick would take him. He was the dad that Christopher never had.

Christopher's mom would often go off the grid, and Nick would always be there to make sure Christopher was fed, clothed, and had a place to stay. They were a sight to see, the two of them. They were both kids. One was just forty years older than the other. Christopher had a baby brother, and eventually Nick stepped in to be dad to him as well.

Nick would come in to order his Con Panna (a double shot of espresso pulled over a dollop of whipped cream), and on one side of him was Christopher, and on the other side was baby brother. Nick would ask me questions about parenting. He was clueless.

"How often do they need to take a bath?"

"Do they need special kinds of toothbrushes?"

"Are they too young to drink coffee?"

"Where do I take them to get a backpack for school?"

Having to live life with two little boys under the age of ten cramped Nick's wild bachelor lifestyle, but he didn't seem to mind too much. It was obvious he loved these boys like they were his own. I built trust with Nick and the boys and offered to help in any way I could.

One summer just before school started back, Nick let us keep Christopher and his younger brother for the weekend. We took them shopping, bought school supplies for Christopher, even took them to church with us on Sunday. They loved it and wanted to come back. That's when Nick started coming to RiverChurch. My girls loved having these little guys around. By this time, our son, Jayden, had come along, but he was a brand-new baby who pretty much only ate, slept, and pooped. Christopher and his little brother were far more interactive, so my three girls stepped right up to play the role of big sisters and sometimes even pretended to be mom.

I loved watching my whole family rally around Nick and the boys. This was ministry, a family type of ministry, but it didn't seem like it. It just seemed natural. Nick had become more than a customer; he had become a friend, a brother who was trying his hardest to love a couple of boys who needed a dad. Now he was a dad who needed a family to support him.

Even after I made my transition from that first coffee shop to later owning my own, I saw Nick and Christopher and the little brother regularly, but over time, I saw them less and less. Then one day Nick blew through the doors of Cadence. Tears in his eyes, cheeks red with anxiety, and with a crack in his voice, he said, "He's gone. They took him, and I can't have him."

4

What If

The natural progression for advancement at that first coffee shop was back bar to cashier, cashier to barista, and after you had spent some time as barista, you were then trusted to open and close and essentially manage in the general manager's absence. I made the advancement over the course of my first year, and in that time, I had truly fallen in love with the world of coffee.

Now in my late thirties, I was learning a new trade and felt like I was experiencing a rebirth. This seemed to be a far cry from what I had studied in college. I graduated with a sociology degree from Lee University, just up the road from Chattanooga, more than a decade earlier. I had lived overseas for four years, been on staff at a growing church in South Alabama, and now I was living in Chattanooga planting and leading a brand-new church. On any given weekday and an occasional Saturday, you would find me at my side gig, behind the bar at a local coffee shop. Kristia still argues that we could have saved ourselves a lot of money by not having to pay back student loans, if I had just learned this trade ten years earlier.

While making coffee seemed to have little to do with the theories of behavioral scientists like Auguste Comte, Max Weber, or Emile Durkheim, I was in a sociologist's dreamworld, standing behind an espresso machine every day. I am a people watcher by nature. Human actions, words, routines, even the ways we present ourselves to the world with our clothes, shoes, and accessories—it all fascinates me. How we interact with one another is equally as fascinating—our gatherings, our conversations, our body language when we sit across from someone else. I find it so amazing that people find some sort of protection or comfort with a ten-ounce coffee mug in their hand. It seems to be a grown-up version of our blankie, our "woobie," or whatever you may have had as a kid to make you feel safe and secure. It's all so interesting for me to watch, and what better place to do that than in a quaint little café in the downtown of my city.

The people who would walk through our doors were also fascinating. Besides the dynamic duo of Nick and Gary, there were the countless other customers with whom I built connections.

Billy came in every morning and every afternoon for his large coffee. He always had exact change and often reminded us that he was "this coffee shop's very first customer."

Rachel was the quiet type; she came in after lunch every day for a soy chai. She was friendly but never had much to say other than a few pleasantries. "Routine" was her middle name. She rarely missed an afternoon visit.

Ed came in midmorning, every morning. His was a dry, a very dry, cappuccino. That meant he wanted almost all foam scooped, not poured, over his espresso. When I would call out his drink and slide it across the counter to him, Ed would take his cappuccino and lightly bob it up and down a couple of times to check the weight. It was his version of quality control. If the cup felt nearly empty, he would smile and in his deep voice say, "Well done!" If it was the least bit too heavy, he would look at you with a raised eyebrow and say, "You've made better." This tall, white-haired man with the deep voice and the expensive suit—this higher-up in the financial world—made me feel like I was standing before the Lord Himself every day, waiting to see if my work was pleasing.

Annie worked at a high-end linen boutique down Market Street. She came in after lunch most days while she was running errands for the boutique. If she liked you, she liked you; if she didn't, you knew it. She had a boisterous laugh and the mouth of a sailor. She lived alone in St. Elmo, a trendy historic neighborhood on the south side of the city. On nights and weekends, she worked at an event hall up on Lookout Mountain. We got along well, shared lots of laughs, and occasionally she would open up and tell me some of her personal details—personal hurts, failed relationships.

I enjoyed all these conversations but began to notice that there seemed to be some greater purpose to my being behind the bar. I didn't just make coffee for these people; I listened to their stories—what they were telling and what they weren't. I could hear hurt and pain, anticipation and anxiety in their words. They were more than just "Large Nonfat Sugar-Free Amaretto Lattes." They were real people, with real stories, who needed to be noticed, heard, and valued.

By this time, RiverChurch was up and running. We were gathering with fifty to seventy-five people every Sunday in a rented space where we seemed to do the typical church thing. We sang, sent kids to Kids' Church, and I preached long sermons every week. It was all very typical. I loved our church family, but something seemed to be missing.

I had grown up in church, and I had seen this institution of society from all sorts of angles—from the pew to the platform, sitting on committees, out front, and behind the scenes.

When we moved to Chattanooga, I felt like the church we were planting needed to look different. Not for the sake of looking different but because I was tired of status quo church; personally, I needed different. The black box stage, lights, smoke machines, hipster band, and "sexy church" just didn't do it for me. I wanted a different church experience for the foreseeable future of my life. I didn't know exactly what that would look like, but two or three years in, the church we had planted seemed to be gravitating right back toward the typical that I wanted to avoid.

In many ways, I felt more fulfilled behind the bar of this coffee shop. On Sundays, I found myself with the healthy—the folks who had it all together, no problems, the "blessed and highly favored." On Monday, I crossed paths with the sick, the broken, the wounded, and the discarded. I wished there was a way that the church I was pastoring and the bar behind which I stood could somehow connect or complement each other. I just didn't know how that would or could ever happen.

Before we left south Alabama, our family traveled back and forth to Chattanooga for several weekend visits. By this time, we had already started dreaming about, seeking counsel for, and planning our move to this city to plant RiverChurch. Our visits to Chattanooga were increasingly filled with wonderings and what-ifs.

I remember one conversation I had with a friend of mine in a Starbucks up the road in Cleveland. From where Jerry and I sat, we could see the steeples of at least a half dozen churches. We sat there, the two of us, equally restless and dissatisfied with what we saw in the American church and asked, "What if the church could actually look different?"

In hindsight, I realize that I had become so accustomed to looking at the church and examining all the things that I thought were wrong with it, I had personally lost sight of Jesus. In fact, my response to what I saw wrong was to do what so many other church planters do—start a new one. It made total sense. Move to a city with more than a thousand churches and plant a new one. But without a clear view of Jesus, where He was, and what He was doing, I kept finding myself in the same cycle of doing what was typical, which led to more frustration and restlessness. I suppose I thought I could just do church better than what I had seen so far. How arrogant was that? What I didn't realize was that this was all part of the larger plan for my life. Jesus was taking two entirely different professions, a pastor and a barista, and merging them together, for no other purpose than to help me truly discover where He was working and to join Him in the process.

On another weekend visit to Chattanooga, we stopped for lunch at a favorite pizza restaurant downtown. I had been reading a book by Mark Batterson, the pastor of National Community Church in Washington, DC. In his book, *In a Pit with a Lion on a Snowy Day*, Batterson tells the story of how his church had opened Ebenezer's Coffeehouse a few blocks over from the United States Capitol. His story inspired me to consider an unrealistic what-if.

As we were loading our family up in our car, I asked Kristia, "What if the church we planted could have a coffee shop connected to it, right here in downtown?"

She politely but briefly entertained my idea with "Yeah, that would be cool."

In my head, I could hear a missile careening through the air and hitting the ground with a hard thud.

OK, well that didn't go like I wanted it to, I thought.

Nothing more was said about it.

We drove back to Alabama never really entertaining the idea again, until …

One afternoon in the summer of 2010, Brian came in and ordered a cup of house coffee in a mug. That meant he intended to stay for a while. It was a Tuesday afternoon, and business seemed uncharacteristically slow. He sat at a table by the front window with a book, and I did my best to be seen and not heard. It seemed like hours went by without a single customer coming in. I had pretty much completed my routine tasks for that shift, so I thought I would check on him to see if he needed anything.

"Are you good, man? Can I refill your coffee?"

"Yeah, that would be great. Thanks." I took his mug behind the bar to refill it and brought it back to his table.

He was doing a Bible study, and the pastor inside of me couldn't be contained. "What are you studying?"

He showed me the book. It was a study of the book of Genesis.

From there, our conversation took on a life of its own.

We instantly connected. Shared stories about our families and compared notes as dads of lots of kids. He had three boys and a girl, and we had three girls and were expecting our boy within the next week. I found myself with a brand-new friend, one who was truly heaven sent.

From there, my conversation with Brian bloomed into a friendship. Three days later, I took my entire family on a blind date to have dinner with his family at their house. Almost every week after that,

Brian would stop by the coffee shop, and we would chat, encourage each other, and build a stronger friendship.

Days, weeks, and months rolled by with numerous conversations about life, family, purpose, and wondering if we were doing what we were created to do. It was January 2011 when Brian brought his wife to the coffee shop for what I suspected might be an afternoon date. As they were having coffee, I walked up to their table to chat a little, but I could tell their discussion was intense. Nothing bad, they weren't fighting or anything, they were just kicking around their own what-ifs.

They invited me into their conversation.

Little did I know that their what-ifs would resurrect my what-if and ultimately lead me to a life-changing discovery.

I was about to find Jesus.

5

Cadence

If I were to tell you, in detail, how Cadence Coffee Company came into existence, I would literally have to write another book. The mind-blowing things that happened to turn a what-if into a "what is" are as numerous as the beans in our hoppers!

One of the most frequently asked questions sent my way is "How did you come up with the name Cadence?"

The origin of the name isn't all that great. We just didn't want a name that sucked.

At the time, Brian was an avid cyclist; he had envisioned a café that would be in an area accessible to Chattanooga's cycling community and thematically styled to appeal to them as well.

Cadence in the world of cycling is the number of completed revolutions per minute at any set speed. Besides having a few bicycle wheels on our walls and a few retro bikes placed around the shop, we never really made much of a splash in that pool.

Webster defines *cadence* as "the beat, time, or measure of rhythmical motion or activity." If you're looking for synonyms, you will find words like "beat," "measure," "meter," or "rhythm." I like that last word the best. It gives me hope that our name was in fact providentially inspired.

Human beings are creatures of habit or ritual. In modern speak, we talk about the rhythms of our lives. My daily rhythm starts at 4:00 a.m., slowly but deliberately centering my heart for the day ahead. By five, I am at the gym. By seven, I am heading into work, getting my first cup of coffee, and then setting about my daily tasks. I head home later in the afternoon and try to catch a ten-minute power nap before I engage with my family for the evening. Now, there are variations to that rhythm, but that's the typical cadence of my day. You have your rhythms as well.

From the first day we opened our doors, Cadence became part of the rhythm of people's lives.

Our first customer was a young, up-and-coming, sharp suit working for Morgan Stanley. He walked in and ordered a double shot of espresso the day before we opened. Our lights were on, all systems were go, a few minor tweaks were needed, and we were ready to pull the string on our open sign the next day. When he walked in, he thought we were already open, so he walked up to the cash register to place his order. We laughed a lot after that day about how he was our first customer before we were even taking customers.

We quickly became part of his cadence. Every morning, he came in and ordered his large nonfat latte, virtually at the same time every day. He eventually stopped telling us what he wanted. He would step up to the register to pay, but we already had his cup in the line of drinks to be made from the moment he walked through the door.

We were part of his rhythm the day he came in to tell us he had proposed to his girlfriend. We were part of his rhythm months later when he was just days away from marrying his girlfriend, now fiancée. When his first baby boy was born, we were still part of his rhythm. You should have seen his face when he came to the door of his wife's hospital room the day after she delivered their baby. He had stayed at the hospital with her, which meant he would miss his usual large nonfat latte. I planned it just right so that about the same time he would normally be walking through our doors, I was at the hospital, knocking on the door to their room. He came to the door—messy hair, morning breath, and all. There I stood in the hallway, his latte in hand.

"Have a great day" were the only words I said before walking down the hall. He was speechless.

I could tell you of countless others who've made us part of their daily cadence. It's cool, but it's more than cool. It's holy. I've come to see the space we hold in the daily rhythm of some of our customers as sacred space. It's as if Jesus Himself stands behind the bar with us, encouraging us.

"You stand right here and consistently, rhythmically, faithfully be part of their everyday lives."

In that place, we have shared in the joys and the tears of countless lives.

We had no clue what significance our name would carry when we decided on the name Cadence. In hindsight, it was somewhat of an obscure prophecy—a declaration of who and what we were to be—a place that was part of the cadence or rhythm of life for others.

I'd be lying if I said at times I wish we had chosen a different name. I've often considered changing it. I suppose I like change. But change will have to come in different ways. I don't see us changing our name any time soon, maybe ever for that matter.

Because Cadence is who we are and who we are to be.

6

CHURCH IN REVERSE

One Tuesday morning, a freshman from UTC (University of Tennessee, Chattanooga) came into the shop. He was a clean-cut guy who seemed to want to get an early start on his day. His wide-eyed smile and friendly voice were uncharacteristic of a college freshman at 6:30 a.m. We exchanged pleasantries as I poured his coffee. Early on in our conversation, Chase began asking questions about my story. This was an odd change for me, as I was typically the one asking these kinds of questions of our customers. I always felt a sense of responsibility to listen to the story of the person on that side of the bar. But in this situation, Chase seemed very intentional in learning more about me and mine.

I don't hide the fact that I'm a pastor or a Christian, but I've discovered that leading off with that information can sometimes kill a conversation before it ever starts. In this conversation, however, it wasn't long before my faith and my calling became a topic of discussion. I remember telling him that I was a pastor and that the coffee shop gig was just my way of putting food on the table for my family. (I hadn't quite come to the realization that the two roles were interconnected. The whole pastorista thing wasn't a concept that I had grasped yet. I'm a slow learner.)

"You're a pastor?" he asked, appearing disappointed.

"I am." I could just hear this conversation coming to a screeching halt.

"That's crazy!" he said in amazement. Suddenly, his eyes lit back up again as his smile stretched across the full breadth of his face.

"When I woke up this morning, I prayed and asked God to direct me today. I literally asked Him to tell me where to go and what He wanted me to do. I felt like I was supposed to come here and 'meet the guy behind the counter.' At least that's what I felt like He told me to do. I assumed He wanted me to come tell you about Jesus, maybe even lead you to know Him. But you already do."

We laughed about the irony, and eventually he sat down with his coffee and spent some time reading, praying, and meditating. This is what I had hoped to see when we had opened Cadence months earlier—a safe space, a sacred space where folks could come and experience a few peaceful minutes with their Creator.

Before he left, we chatted a little more. He asked about the church we had planted. I asked about his freshman year and his studies. He was an up-and-coming leader for a campus ministry, looking forward to being placed in a local high school later that semester. As an official leader in that ministry, Chase would have the opportunity to meet with and mentor younger students, and he couldn't wait. A few more minutes passed, and soon he was off to his first class for the day.

Sunday eventually rolled around and with it our weekly time to gather at our little rented church building. Just before our gathering started, I walked into our auditorium, surprised to discover Chase sitting in the middle of a row with what I presumed to be ten or twelve of his closest college friends on either side of him. I was almost as giddy as my young daughters, who were completely enthralled by this batch of good-looking college guys who had walked in that Sunday morning. I had no expectation after our conversation earlier in the week that Chase would be coming to our gathering, or that he intended to bring a group of friends with him, but we were all pleasantly surprised.

That was the first of many gatherings I shared with this group of students committed to and passionate in their relationship with Jesus. Every Thursday morning, they showed up at Cadence at 5:00 a.m., an hour and a half before we opened, to pray together. (Yeah, you read that right … 5:00 a.m. … college students … prayer. I know, right?) I provided the space each week, and they brought the heat. Their passion and love for God was inspiring and convicting. For the rest of that semester, and well into the fall semester, Cadence was their place to come and hang out, study, and pray together. RiverChurch also became their home church during those semesters, and I couldn't have been happier. I felt like a proud dad.

That same fall, we started a gathering at Cadence on Saturday nights, which we creatively called Saturday Church. We had acoustic worship. I brought a teaching, and afterward, we encouraged people to go out and about downtown and simply meet folks and invite them back for a cup of coffee.

Our objective was twofold.

Firstly, we wanted to move toward the students who lived on campus. We had a decent group coming on Sunday mornings, but I imagined that if we had a gathering closer to the university campus, we would draw even more.

Secondly, we wanted to experience church in reverse. I had a buddy who loved coffee and faith even more than I do. He offered me a phrase in one of our coffee conversations that stuck with me.

"Shannon, I think what you have here is a perfect opportunity for church in reverse. For too long, the church has expected people to come to it, but what if God wants the church to go to where people are? Because let's face it. Fewer and fewer are coming to church every Sunday."

Michael was the church bartender at the megachurch he attended in Birmingham. He was the guy who ran the coffee bar in the lobby of his local church. He probably could have served in any area of ministry, but he loved standing behind the bar of that little café every Sunday. He said that was where he was able to connect and hear the stories of folks who would stop by for their java with Jesus.

This was where things started to make sense. It was becoming more and more clear that Jesus wanted us to be less worried about getting butts in seats on Sunday mornings and more concerned about getting butts—ours—out the doors of the church into the streets of our city where people were.

Saturday Church was our first real step in the direction of experiencing church in reverse. Within weeks, we discovered that the people who were gathering with us weren't the people we had hoped to attract at all. I remember looking around the café one Saturday night just before Christmas to see a sea of homeless people who had begun gathering with us for worship each week. In fact, there were way more of them than there were of us.

We started providing food after our gatherings. What began as bagged sandwiches and chips morphed into full-on meals, and before long, other folks from the city were bringing food and helping us serve. Small groups, Sunday school classes, and other churches came with loads of food to serve—and the people and the homeless people just kept coming. This was church in reverse.

Don't get me wrong. It was hard. Some Saturday nights, folks would come in drunk and get into arguments with each other right in the middle of my sermon. We'd have to usher them out, calm them down, and get them some food before we sent them back to their camps.

One night, we had six cop cars outside the café, all because Gary was ticked off at his son, Michael, and Michael's girlfriend. They thought it would be OK to air out their family grievances right there in front of God and everyone in the middle of my teaching on the Sermon on the Mount.

We mourned together when we learned that Wanda had died alone of an overdose in her government-subsidized studio apartment.

Sometimes on Saturday nights, the room smelled, and we went home smelling like menthol cigarettes and cheap liquor, simply because it's what the people we hung out with smelled like.

This was a far cry from the cool, hip, college student scene that I had hoped we would create. Yet it became very apparent that this was where Jesus was and where He was leading us as a community of faith.

Later that year, the lease on our church building ended, and we chose not to renew. As a new year began, RiverChurch found itself in a strangely similar situation with many of our new friends—homeless. A lot of the folks who had previously called RiverChurch their home didn't make the transition with us—for lots of reasons. But as 2014 began, so, too, began a new season for RiverChurch. Our family and the fraction of folks who stuck with us stepped into a new season and into a new place that we didn't see coming.

Our family moved downtown to a rental house, where we saw a lot more of our homeless friends on a regular basis. One morning, I walked out my front door to find Mark Underbridge sitting on our porch swing with a box of doughnuts that he had finagled from a stranger. Mark filled out a guest card one night at Saturday Church, indicating that his last name was Underbridge because … well, he camped under a bridge. I was quite surprised and a little amused when I stepped out on our front porch that morning to find Mr. Underbridge stuffing his face with chocolate glazed doughnuts. He raised his eyebrows, cheeks full of food as he offered me a half grin and an outstretched box of nearly destroyed doughnuts.

This was never what we saw coming when we hauled everything we owned to Chattanooga in a twenty-six-foot horse trailer five years earlier. But what we had stumbled upon by God's providence was the very thing we had been looking for—not church as usual: Sunday-morning programs, lights, and all the bells and whistles.

No, this was different. A distinctively different kind of church experience. It was smelly, dirty, and sometimes scary and uncertain, but this was church in reverse.

7

No Accidents

That day Nick came into Cadence in a frantic state was a day that would change a lot of lives for a very long time. Earlier that morning, Christopher had been surrendered to the state. Months earlier, his mom had taken him and his younger brother to a nearby hotel, where she met up with some of her acquaintances.

No one really knows what happened that night, but young Christopher called Nick from the hotel and asked him to come get him and baby brother. He couldn't tell Nick exactly where he was; he could only describe what he saw from the hotel window. Mom had passed out on the bed, and so had her squad. The boys sat alone, awake, and afraid, hoping someone would come find them, and eventually Nick did.

Mom went to jail, and a few days later, her sisters stepped up and agreed to take in her boys. One sister took the baby brother, and another sister took Christopher. This was the living arrangement for a few short months until the aunt with whom Christopher was living decided she couldn't do it anymore. So one cold February morning, she took him to court, where he was surrendered into the custody of the state of Tennessee. Nick was in the courtroom that morning as young Christopher was escorted by a bailiff out of the room. He spoke up, asking the judge to let him take him, but when the judge learned that he had no biological tie to Christopher, he politely asked Nick to be seated and stay quiet. It was at that point that Nick ran from the courtroom straight into the doors of Cadence.

The door flew open as this big, broad-shouldered, tough-as-nails bounty hunter stepped through with tears pouring down his face.

"I've lost him."

He explained what had happened in court that morning and eventually left in absolute desperation. As he left, I continued to make cappuccinos and lattes for customers who had no clue that somewhere a little boy's world was spiraling out of control. As I stood behind the machine, I knew I couldn't just be a spectator. I had to do something and do it fast.

"Jesus, I know that You are here. Please give me wisdom. What can we do? What would You do?"

Almost immediately, I remembered that a RiverChurch family member worked for the Department of Children's Services, so I called her.

"You're calling about Christopher, aren't you?" she asked.

"How did you know?"

She had met Christopher at church, and in her role with DCS, she was part of the intake process when a child came into foster care.

"I'm looking at his picture right now. I'm having to enter his information into the system so he can be assigned to a foster family."

"How do we become a foster family?"

She explained that it might be difficult, but maybe we had a chance. At three o'clock that afternoon, we met Christopher's case worker at our house. She walked through for an emergency home evaluation and interview of our entire family. She took our information and sent it off to Nashville for a variety of background checks that all came back clear. At five o'clock that evening, we walked into the DCS offices, and on the second-floor mezzanine, looking over the rails into the lobby, was young Christopher.

"How did you find me?"

It was as if he had been looking, hoping for a familiar face to walk through those doors to rescue him. That night, we took him home, and our journey as foster parents officially began. Over the six months that he stayed with us, we discovered that Christopher had needs that we were not equipped to meet. The trauma and abuse to which he had been exposed was nothing any of us knew about on the front end when we became an emergency placement. However, over time, we began to see signs that pointed to a dark past that this kid had lived through, and he desperately needed a family and a living environment that had been trained and equipped to help him deal with life.

The Department of Children's Services decided to place Christopher with a different family that could offer him the help he needed. The day he left, even with six of us in our house, it still felt empty, quiet, and so very sad. Kristia and I had many conversations afterward about our future as foster parents, and we ultimately decided to keep our home open and just wait for the time we would get another call. And a few months later, that call came.

We were asked to go to a nearby hospital that afternoon, where we were met by a nurse and a caseworker. They escorted us to an empty hospital room, and a few minutes later, a brand-new baby boy was rolled into the room. They told us his name and explained that the circumstances surrounding his coming into state custody were quite complicated. The parents were unstable and potentially violent, so we were instructed to leave the hospital that day as "naturally" as possible.

"Act like brand-new parents," they said.

We were escorted to our car with a security guard and a nurse scouring the parking lot for the birth father; they feared he might be outside, and they wanted to avoid an altercation. As they described the birth dad, I noticed that his unique description matched one of the homeless guys we had met at Saturday Church.

Six months earlier, this guy's girlfriend walked up to me, patting her stomach.

"Preacher, I'm pregnant!"

"You are? How exciting? So … what are you going to do? You're camping, right?"

We had learned that most homeless folks in Chattanooga preferred to see their homelessness as camping.

"We'll be all right. My baby daddy is gettin' a job, and we'll be fine."

"I'll pray that happens for you guys. Can I pray for you now?"

She was more than willing to let me pray. In fact, she patted her slightly rounded stomach again.

"Pray for my baby too." So, I did.

I laid my hands on her stomach and prayed for her and her baby that would be born later that year and asked God to protect them both and to keep a watchful eye on them in the weeks, months, and years ahead.

Months later, as Kristia and I sat with a newborn baby boy on our living room floor, we unwrapped his blanket and looked at the hospital bracelet on his ankle to find that this baby was the very same baby I prayed for six months earlier, in his mother's womb.

We were mind blown. Only God knew that there was the slightest, thinnest, most insignificant connection between us and this baby. We were part of the answer to the very prayer I prayed that night at Saturday Church. We named him Noa, a nickname and an acronym for the fact that with God there are No Accidents.

We had Noa for nearly a year in our house. We actually thought we would adopt him. But Noa wasn't to be ours. His birth grandmother eventually reappeared, and the state eventually awarded her full custody. The day he left our house was truly one of the darkest days in the history of our family. It felt like we had experienced a death of a child, only we were limited in our ability to fully and publicly grieve the loss. We've never personally experienced the death of a child, but we have several friends who have. Noa was fully alive and living less than a mile away, but we had an empty bed in our house, and the loss was deep and real.

A few months later, DCS called us again to bring home a two-month-old baby girl who would eventually become our daughter, making us a party of seven.

The journey that started the day Nick busted through our doors was one filled with high highs and super-low lows. There were lots of tears, lots of fears, and very hard moments along the way. But the journey that started with Nick and led us to Christopher, then later to Noa, and eventually to our beautiful Arielle Tikvah, was a journey that still reminds us today that with God, there truly are no accidents.

8

REAL PEOPLE

We never really set out to specifically work with the homeless when we opened Cadence. Our core values of coffee, community, and change compelled us to use a hot drink to build an environment that would positively impact people in our city, regardless of any label they wore. One of my favorite T-shirts that we sold from our merchandise wall said, "Everyone deserves a great cup of coffee." That's why, on any given day, if you walk through the doors of Cadence, you will find people from every walk of life—rich, poor, black, white, and every color of pigmentation in between—having coffee. We serve nice folks, mean folks, religious folks, rebellious folks, gay folks, straight folks, and folks who claim no orientation at all. We serve people who drive nice cars and who live in nice houses, and we serve people who have no car or who have no house to call their home.

Our relationship with the homeless community started rather organically and largely because of Saturday Church. When we started gathering on Saturday nights at Cadence, we made bagged lunches and gave them to anyone who was hungry or needing food. But something didn't seem right about that. It felt staged, unnatural, and uncomfortable to have them stand in a line and wait for someone to hand them some food, while the rest of us "do-gooders" stood around smiling with cheesy grins.

It was a kind statement of gratitude that changed my perspective on how we were helping homeless folks in our city on Saturday nights.

"Thanks for feeding us."

Annette was grateful. I knew she was; I could see it in her toothless smile. Her plate was loaded with food—fried chicken, baked beans, potato salad, and a mess of desserts. This poor woman had very little else to smile about, but in that moment, she was happy. But her statement bothered me.

These people weren't animals that we were herding through a line, throwing food at them. They weren't children scooting through a cafeteria line where sour-faced curmudgeons in hairnets growled, "Whattaya want?" while slinging slop on their trays. These people were people with names, feelings, some level of dignity, and most of all they had stories to tell—and they needed someone to listen. Truthfully, like most of us, they needed to know that someone saw them not as homeless, or poor, or addicted, or as an alcoholic, but that someone truly cared for them and wanted to hear their stories. So, we stopped feeding them and started eating with them.

Our kids caught on too! Homeless folks weren't some life form that we tried to avoid; they were real people, and in some cases, larger than life.

One Saturday night, an old man sat on the sidewalk outside of Cadence while we gathered for Saturday Church. He was cold and had been drinking earlier in the evening to stay warm, so we invited him in and offered him a cup of coffee. He accepted the invitation. He was a quiet, white-bearded old man who stayed bundled up in his coat and hat while he sat content on a couch in the back of the room. It wasn't long before my energetic three-year-old son came bounding by him, threw up a friendly little wave, and then stopped dead in his tracks for a double take.

"Santa Claus?" he asked in complete astonishment.

Drunk or sober, I'm not sure, but the old man responded on the spot with a matter of fact yes, and for the rest of the evening, Jayden sat on the couch talking to him like an old friend. He asked about Mrs. Claus, the reindeer, and how they all flew. He even gave him his Christmas list, which at the time was only three things:

A bike for himself.
A bike for me.
A gift for his little friend Kiyana.

He couldn't believe it. Santa had come to Saturday Church. Jay was so overwhelmed with excitement that he went running around the room, making sure everyone else knew that we had a special guest among us.

"Santa Claus is here! Go tell him what you want for Christmas!"

Some folks walked over with Jayden to meet the rather conspicuous old elf. Others just told Jayden what they wanted, and he gladly relayed the message, running between the "naughty" and the "nice" to old Kris Kringle, telling him what everyone wanted for Christmas. The old man played right along. He never indicated that he was anyone other than Santa Claus himself.

When it came time for Santa to leave, Jay wanted to follow him outside to see if he would fly away with his reindeer. But Santa encouraged him to stay inside where it was warm and told him to be good and he would see him later.

Jayden's night was officially made.

The feeling was mutual. The old man, somewhat sobered and deeply impacted, told us as he left, "That kid made my day."

I know he's my kid, but that night, a three-year-old kid looked at a drunk, homeless, old man and saw a legend. He didn't see him for what he was but for what he could be—a symbol of hope, joy, and cheer. He sat easily with this man for three-quarters of an hour, making him feel like he had value and worth for that entire amount of time.

As I tucked Jay into bed later that night, I could tell he was still thinking about Santa Claus.

"Dad, Santa Claus really is a nice man. He was very nice to talk to."

Then he smiled, closed his eyes, and went off to sleep with visions of sugar plums dancing in his head.

I kind of wonder if "Santa" didn't do the very same thing that night.

Now, I'm not advocating that you let your three-year-old go hang out with the drunk guy on the street corner downtown. Some folks would never feel comfortable having their kids in that kind of environment. Trust me, we've sure had the questions come our way …

"Are you sure that is safe?"

No. It's not safe, and I understand the concern. I am truly thankful Jayden didn't come home that night asking for a bottle of Chattanooga whiskey to be left in his stocking for Christmas.

"How can you feel good about putting your kids in *that* environment with *those* people?"

My answer: "How can I *not* put my kids in that kind of environment?" This is exactly what the Author my faith would do.

Jesus loved the unlovable. He befriended the friendless. He ate with outcasts.

He saw people as people—not homeless, not poor, not an addict, not a prostitute, a thief, or a criminal.

My job as a parent, if I'm truly following the example of Jesus and want my kids to do the same, is to teach them to do the same not just with words but with actions. The good thing is that kids are easy to teach this kind of lesson. I'm always fascinated how children rarely look at other children and immediately begin to label them according to their skin color, socioeconomic class, or where they live. It's the grown-ups who come along with the labels, putting our filters on others, and we teach our kids to see the world through those filters.

Please don't read what I'm about to tell you and think I'm bragging on us as parents. Our kids maybe but not us. They got it. They understood the importance of seeing people without filters, and it's a lesson they live by even now. To this day, my girls will often sit around the dinner table and talk about their "homeless friends."

My older kids often work behind the bar at Cadence, and they have come home many days with their own stories of the folks they serve each day. Sure, there are the "cute guy" stories or the "this girl had on the cutest skirt today" conversation. But it's the stories of their conversations with their homeless friends that I love the most.

"I love Paul; he's such a sweet man."

"Jim was a stinker today; he tried to trick me into giving him another free cup of coffee after he had already gotten one Pay It Forward and then a refill."

"Grady told me that I make his coffee better than anyone else at Cadence. He just says that because I put a cup of sugar in it!"

If you didn't know any better, you would think they were talking about someone their age or someone they hang out with daily. I suppose on some level, they do hang out with these people daily, and my kids love them, and they feel that the feeling is mutual.

One lady told us one time, "We like coming here because you treat us like real people." There's a reason for that: they *are* real people. We don't have to be afraid of them, and we're willing to get dirty in the process of doing life together.

If we truly want to make a difference in the lives of other people, we would do well to learn from kids and simply see people as people—real people. That's what Jesus did. That's what Jesus would do.

9

Normal

"How ya doin', Sam?"

"Normal."

Thus begins my usual conversation when Sam comes to Cadence for his twelve-ounce medium roast, all black. He pulls out two one-dollar bills and his loyalty card so we can give it one more of the ten punches he needs to earn a free cup of coffee. He's probably earned fifty free cups of coffee by now. He's been coming in for years.

He lives in a subsidized high-rise on the south side of town. He walks several blocks every day to come spend a few hours sitting at a table with his laptop. Some days he plays games, some days he scrolls through Facebook, and occasionally he brings his laptop up to the counter to show us the latest meme that's made him laugh.

He's a well-read, smart individual. He would tell you that he's more of a smart aleck than smart. While most people see religion and politics as the two death traps for any conversation, Sam sees them as an afternoon stroll in the park. If you're willing to talk about religion, politics, or double A baseball, Sam is in. He's a Christ follower, a former member of the Church of Christ, a true-blue

Democrat, and a seasonal employee for the Chattanooga Lookouts Baseball organization.

I wish I was as smart as Sam gives me credit, because he often assumes I know a lot more than I really do.

"Sam, how ya feeling about the upcoming mayoral election?"

"Don't ask. You should already know how I feel." He then offers a verbal op-ed as to why one candidate is a joke and why the other is getting his vote. He has talked to both, read up on their political platforms, and has solidly come to his decision as to who he is voting for and why.

He'll generally make some sort of cheeky statement about our political differences, and then he laughs.

"You knew I was going to say that."

I didn't really.
I never know what he's going to say next.

Still, I'll laugh right along with him.

Our friendship has survived two presidential elections, which is more than some of his former friends on social media can say. During a recent election, he had lots to say. He would post, share, or like certain political commentary on social media, and inevitably he would get pushback from a friend, a fellow church member, or a family member, and he would come in slightly perturbed at their responses. He's not obnoxious about his views, but he doesn't put up with obnoxious either.

"Shannon, you know me, and you know I just won't tolerate that kind of ridiculousness, so I blocked them."

"I know, Sam, I know."

When politicians say or do something questionable or disagreeable, Sam comes in with guns ablaze.

"I told you! I told you this would happen. You know good and well that I said when they got elected that they would do this, didn't I? Didn't I call it before it happened?"

"Yes, Sam, you sure did."

Sometimes I don't know or remember that he said it would happen, but he assumes I do, so I agree with him just to see where the conversation goes.

I don't argue with him. I just listen.

He just needs space to air his grievances with political powers, Christians who don't represent Jesus very well, or a family member who's getting on his nerves.

When he leaves, I tell him, "Be good, Sam."

He responds with a blunt "No."

When I'm leaving the café and he's still there, I say, "See ya later, Sam."

He quips back, "Thanks for the warning."

Sam's wife fell ill a few years ago and was hospitalized for several days. His daily rhythm consisted of a late-morning visit to the hospital to check on her, then an afternoon stop by the café for his usual cup of coffee. Cadence was solidly part of his daily rhythm, and wild horses wouldn't keep him from that rhythm.

When his world was upside down and spinning out of control, he needed something, some place that he could go to find just a little bit of normal. We've all had times when things seemed out of control, and we've longed for a little normal.

Kacey and Michael were morning regulars at Cadence. Their drink of choice was an almond-milk-chai-extra-cinnamon, and their usual spot was the couch in the front of the café. They sat there for a few minutes every morning before they had to go their separate ways to work. They always seemed like newlyweds. They laughed and talked, the ideal picture of what a happy couple should be. They came by on Saturdays, and Michael enjoyed chatting with Sam. When we started gathering again for worship on Sunday mornings, although Cadence was officially closed, Kacy and Michael would come in and sit on the café side and have their almond-milk-chai-extra-cinnamon while we gathered for worship in the adjacent room.

During a thanksgiving trip to the beach one year, Michael suffered a medical emergency out in the water. Kacey tried to save him, but he didn't survive. She messaged one of our baristas the day after it happened to tell us that Michael had passed away unexpectedly. Our entire staff was devastated. How could this happen? Weeks later, we hosted a memorial gathering for Michael at Cadence. Scores of people stopped by Kacey and Michael's normal hangout to grieve and share memories together.

Even now, though Michael isn't with her, Cadence is part of Kacey's normal morning routine. She calls ahead now. It's still too hard to come in and sit without him. When her name pops up on the caller ID, we forgo the usual "Thanks for calling Cadence" and go straight to "Hey, Kacey, you coming for your almond-milk-chai-extra-cinnamon?" Normal for her doesn't look like it used to, but somehow, she found a new normal, and thankfully we're still part of it.

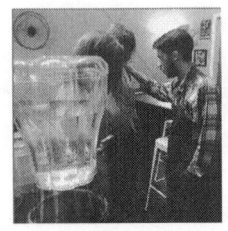

I'll never forget the day Sam walked in to tell us that his wife had passed away the night before. Our crew behind the bar that morning did what was normal for us. They stepped around the bar, encircled Sam, and prayed for comfort for his heart.

Even after his wife passed away, Sam kept his daily routine of coming to Cadence. He never said much to anyone about what he was feeling or the loneliness he experienced after she was gone. He confided in me, and I knew he missed her. But if you were a regular customer sitting in the shop when he came in, you would hear him respond the same way every time when we asked how he was doing: "Normal."

The days and weeks that followed his wife's death seemed to get even harder for Sam. He had to change apartments and found himself with almost no furniture; life was tough. Still, he came—every day—to Cadence for his coffee.

When people like Sam and Kacey experience loss, sometimes the hardest thing in the world is to know what to say or do for them. As we walked through dark days with them and others, we found that the most benevolent thing we could do was to be present and offer normal to them. Our daily being there, ready to serve, was a simple and subtle picture of exactly where and what Jesus would be and do. He would offer a place, a routine, an outlet—something familiar that would allow them to see that life continues to move forward; the planet keeps spinning, and He would assure them that they weren't going to fall off. That's what He wanted us to do—give them a little bit of normal.

It was a year to the day after Sam's wife passed away that we hosted a Good Friday night of worship and reflection at Cadence. The lights were dim. Candles were lit. We had created the perfect environment for people to carefully and quietly remember the death, burial, and resurrection of Jesus.

The music started, and everyone started to sing. Suddenly from among the crowd in the room, a booming baritone voice climbed up far above all the others. With his best attempt to harmonize and a significant amount of vibrato, Sam's voice permeated the room. Sam's church didn't use instruments as part of their worship, so he was accustomed to using his voice as an instrument—and He did.

It caught some folks by surprise. Some were even startled a little as Sam belted out his first few notes. Undaunted by the giggles of a couple of kids nearby, Sam sang anyway. He sang every song, familiar or unfamiliar, louder, bolder, and stronger than anyone else in the room.

No one in the room knew that this was the first anniversary of his wife's death. He missed her terribly. But he knew where she was.

"This Good Friday was an especially Good Friday for her," he told me later. "She's seeing Him face-to-face."

Sam's wife had found her new normal; Sam had found his, and I realized that night that Cadence had found its new normal too. This was just one of the many reasons why we had been placed at 11 East Seventh Street—for people like Sam and Kacey and countless others. In good times and in bad, we were to be a place where they could go. We were to be friends who welcomed them in, to offer them a smile, a little encouragement and hope, a place where they could find and feel normal.

10

Lower the Bar

Mondays are universally tough for just about anyone who enjoys a two-day weekend.

Tough to get up.
Tough to get going.
Tough to get out the door.
Tough to get back to the grind.
Tough to feel motivated to walk into a new week and face it head-on.

The local coffee shop can become a minute clinic where you run in and grab a caffeine fix before you must walk into work and are forced to play nice for the rest of the day.

As a barista, you're fine with that; you don't really expect folks to walk through your door all smiles and giggles at six thirty in the morning. Our expectations of folks aren't really that high on Mondays. But occasionally, you get a customer who, for them, it's Monday—all day, every day.

Maybe they don't do mornings, or maybe they're perpetually having a bad day for the duration of their life. That's how Saul was. Every time he walked into the shop, his countenance was always the same—never a smile, always a scowl. I'm convinced that if he were to smile, his face would crack. Confession: every time Saul walked through the door, the little voice in my head would say, "Oh boy, here comes Mr. Grumpy."

I hated waiting on him. No matter how positive, how complimentary, how kind, how nongrumpy I tried to be, he never reciprocated. He always walked through the door, up to the counter, and mumbled, "Small coffee."

Then, as if he were standing at a wishing well, he would throw two dollars across the counter at me or whoever was taking his order. Sometimes he didn't have two dollars, so he would throw a five note at me, and I'd pick it up and pull out his three in change and throw them back across the counter at him. I know … I know. I probably shouldn't have, but if I struggle with anything, I struggle with rude people, and he was, in my humble opinion, the grown-up poster child for rudeness.

Then there was Randall. He had a reputation with the staff. They hated to see him come. Typically, he would fiercely swing the door open, then come barreling up to the counter with his own travel mug.

"Good morning" was our usual greeting from behind the bar.

On his side of the bar? Crickets. Nothing. Not a smile or any sort of acknowledgment. He just plopped his cup down, expecting us to magically know what he wanted.

If I was behind the bar, I seemed to get a little more interaction with him, but the employees always felt like he saw them as subservient, "the help," and they labeled him the "world's rudest customer to ever live on the planet." That's not a title to be coveted.

Randall, Saul, and others like them stood in stark contrast to the bright rays of sunshine who would walk through the doors. It didn't matter if it was Monday or Friday, if their week was going well or if it was tanking, these were the ones whose cup was always half-full of happiness before the first drop of coffee ever hit the bottom of it.

Gail worked for an attorney, and her job could be stressful, but not a day went by that she didn't walk through the door with a smile as she ordered her small medium roast with room for cream. She particularly enjoyed being served by college guys, who were her junior by quite a few years.

"I'm Gail. They probably warned you about me," she'd tell them. Then she would giggle.

Gail always knew how to take the lemons life gave her and make lemonade. She came in later than normal one day. She had been to the courthouse for the final signing of her divorce papers. She was a little less sunshine that morning. A tear trickled down her face as she told me that her marriage was over. I stepped around the bar to hug her. I could see the pain in her eyes. But not for long. She quipped off some sideways comment about her ex.

"Oh well, he wasn't that good a kisser anyway."

She laughed, but I could tell it hurt a little.

Sitting beside her at the bar was Robert, a family law attorney. He was a tough old bull, a veteran soldier and police officer, a tough-as-nails kind of guy. He was a nonfat mocha drinker. And if you were the poor unfortunate soul that made his mocha with whole milk, he would hand it back to you to make it over. He wanted what he paid for, and even though there was no price difference between the two, if he paid for a nonfat mocha, then a nonfat mocha was what he expected. He wasn't really what you would call a ray of sunshine. He gave Mr. Grumpy and Randall a run for their money on the rude customer race. But he occasionally would crack a smile and offer a bit of comic relief to the rest of us. That typically happened when he took out an opponent on one of the video games he played on his cell phone while sitting at the bar.

"What a goofball," he would pop off.

The room would look at him, wondering who he was talking about, and he would point at his phone and clarify, "Oh, it's a guy I'm playing against here on my phone."

Some of my favorite customers always came in as a group. One quartet of laughter was Jason, Russell, Tonya, and Shannon. They were all higher-level executives in town. They were after-lunch coffee drinkers. They were like a moving party—laughing, joking, and teasing each other. When they left, they left whoever was standing behind the bar laughing. Jason was the ringleader. He was the boss of the entire company. He's the same age as me. If he and I had been in school together, we would have stayed in trouble. He always had a joke, a prank, or at least a funny story of how he had played a trick on Tonya, his assistant, or someone else at his office. Their joy was contagious. When Jason took a promotion, he ended up moving away, and the band of merriment dissolved, and that was truly one of the saddest days in Cadence history.

I've learned so much from customers like these. The good ones, the bad ones, the rude ones, and the ones who naturally bring a smile to your face.

I've learned that we are all part of one race really—humanity. Which means we all breathe the same air, experience the same emotions, live in the same world, hear the same news, and learn to deal with the same sorts of circumstances in drastically different ways.

One day when Mr. Grumpy, Saul, came in the shop, Leslie, our cashier, made an insightful observation. "That man always seems so sad. It's almost like he has the weight of the world on his shoulders."

Her perspective changed the way I looked at him. Until that moment, I had never really stopped to consider why he seemed so grumpy. Suddenly, I realized that there might be issues in his life that affected him so drastically he simply cannot smile or return a word of kindness.

I knew of some of the life struggles that Randall faced. He was a dad whose kid had made some bad life choices and was dealing with the consequences of those life choices. Randall had been directly affected by those choices, and while he never spoke of them openly, I know that his circumstances affected how he lived his life and interacted with others.

I had an old friend named Gene who used to come in a couple times a week and have a cup of coffee with me at Cadence. He was much older than me, which meant he had a lot more life experience than I did. One time as I was complaining to Gene about how someone had frustrated me, Gene gave me this advice: "Shannon, people are always going to disappoint you. It's a given. The best thing you can do is lower the bar. Don't have expectations that are too high for them so that when they do disappoint you, it won't hurt so bad."

I took his advice to heart, and I began to give people the space and the grace to be human, to disappoint, or to be rude even. Alexander Pope said it this way, "To err is human; to forgive, divine."

The entire message of the Gospel of Jesus revolves around grace and forgiveness. Every human being who has ever lived has needed grace and forgiveness at some point in their lives. We all have bad days, and we all need people to give us the space to have those bad days. This is what Jesus does for us, and He calls us to do the same.

I don't know what's happening in the lives of the people on the other side of the bar. I don't know what they've lived through in the past or are living through in the present. Life puts so many expectations on all of us; the last thing Saul, Randall, Robert, or anyone else needed was my piddly little expectations for them to say please and thank you. They needed me to lower my bar and extend some grace.

I also learned to appreciate the Gails, Jasons, Russells, Tanyas, and Shannons (not me, another Shannon). I welcomed them into my day because they made up for the kindness, joy, and sometimes, basic human decency that others might not be able to give. I truly learned to be thankful for the nice folks and to pray harder for the mean folks.

I am also more aware of how I interact with the person serving me when they are behind the bar. I have bad days. I'm not always a ray of sunshine. I have Mondays just like everyone else, and my bad day isn't the fault of the barista. I need grace too. I need someone to lower the bar for me. Jesus did.

11

Epic

"I hate white people!"

He didn't mince words. Michael walked into Cadence one Saturday night, slumped down in a chair at a table in the back of the café, crossed his arms, and simply fumed. He was a young black man in his mid-thirties who had aged out of the foster system. An avid gamer who perpetually lived in a world of virtual reality, he loved *Star Trek* and anime, and if he wasn't mad at you, he would talk your head off about all things video games. I got to know all of this and so much more about him over time, but that first encounter, well, it was quite an introduction.

He had been in a verbal altercation with a lady who happened to be white, and in the heat of the moment, that was the distinguishing characteristic about her that seemed to make him the maddest. Some of the RiverChurch family had gathered at the shop that Saturday night when Michael walked in, and they offered him a piece of pizza, which he gladly accepted. As the night went on, Michael cooled off and ended up laughing and having a good time with this group of white folks.

Michael would come occasionally for church and participate in worship. He seemed to legitimately enjoy being around all our church family. One Sunday morning, Preston, our keyboard player, had closed his eyes and raised his single hand during worship. Michael walked past him to get to his seat and slapped Preston's hand with a solid and resounding high five. It startled Preston a little, but he did have his hand in the air, and Michael wasn't about to leave him hanging.

Some Sundays, Michael would offer to help me preach my sermon. I'd be passionately making a point, driving it home, feeling a keen sense of the Holy Spirit's blessing on the words coming out of my mouth, and Michael would raise his hand to add to my point. The first time or two it happened, I'd stop and let him speak, and then I learned how to politely say, "Let me talk right now, Michael." He'd put his hand down and acknowledge my request.

"Oh ... yeah ... OK ... my bad ... you go ahead."

He was a fully animated character—loud, with a laugh that was more like a never-ending cackle that would go on and on and on without him taking a breath.

If given the opportunity, he would testify every Sunday.

"When I came here, I hated white people. I did. They made me mad. I was full of anger, and rage, and hate. But these people ... they are epic. They showed me Jesus, and now I'm a new man."

Epic. That was Michael's word for everything. But there was, in fact, a visible change in him, and it was truly epic.

One Sunday, Michael arrived at church in time for a preservice prayer time. Glynis, one of our church members, was leading the pregathering prayer time. She provided two-ounce cups of anointing oil for the prayer team to walk around and anoint tables, and surfaces, and doorways, praying for God's blessing over the entire space. I happened to be talking to a couple while the prayer team was milling around, anointing and praying, when Michael walked by me with his two ounces of olive oil.

"Whatcha doin', man?" I asked him.

Unimpressed by this new and strange assignment that Glynis had given him, Michael responded, "Anointing junk!"

He walked back through a few minutes later, with a completely empty two-ounce cup. To this day, I have no clue where he put all that oil. I just know he must have anointed a whole lot of ... "junk."

I truly believe Michael experienced life change during the time he was with us, but he was still always a little rough around the edges.

During our month-and-a-half COVID-19 shutdown, we did some sprucing up at Cadence—painted walls, added some plants, and just brightened the place up a little bit.

When Michael saw the changes for the first time, he was in shock. He slung the door open as he walked in, jaw on the floor, and, oblivious to the room full of customers, exclaimed, "What? What in the world has happened in here?"

He's a work in progress.

Michael wasn't homeless; he lived with roommates. His roommates were apparently as passionate about playing video games as he was.

According to him, they would play for days, without stopping to eat, or sleep, or even bathe. On more than one occasion, I had to have a tough love conversation with him.

"Man, what have you been doing? When is the last time you took a bath?"

He'd smile at me sheepishly and say, "I don't know. It's been a while I guess."

We bought him some bodywash, some shampoo, and some laundry detergent, a lot of it in fact, and we kept a supply of it on hand for him. When he ran out at home, all he had to do was come in and let us know, and we'd send him home with more.

When he used it, he would come to Cadence smiling from ear to ear, wanting to show us that he had bathed and that he "looked good." It always seemed to be feast or famine for him. Sometimes he smelled like he hadn't touched a bar of soap for a week, and other times he smelled like he had used an entire bottle in one bathing. Regardless of how he smelled, we loved him, and he knew it.

One day he came into Cadence to tell us about a tense situation with some of his roommates. Apparently, things had gotten so bad at home that he didn't even want to go home at night. Michael was trying to follow Jesus, but his living arrangements often tested his faith to an extreme. He would come in so overwhelmed with frustration with his roommates that he was tempted to literally take matters into his own hands. We'd offer him a cup of coffee and some food to eat. We would pray for him until he was calm again, and off he would go.

This day that Michael came to Cadence, he flung the door open wide in typical Michael fashion. "P.S., you gotta hear what happened!" (P.S. was his shortened form of Pastor Shannon.)

The night before, the roommate who had caused Michael such stress walked up to him and said, "Man, I gotta let all this hate go! I'm sorry for all I've done!"

"You do gotta let that hate go, dawg, 'cause if you don't, it leaves a door open for the devil to come all up in yo bidness!"

At RiverChurch, we seek to be followers of Jesus more than we are Christians. I know it sounds like semantics, but lots of people call themselves Christians, but one who truly follows Christ is an apprentice of Christ. A true Christ follower lives life with Jesus, lives like Jesus, and does what Jesus did. For us, this is what discipleship looks like. We wanted Michael to have a clear picture of Jesus anytime he was around us, and now Michael was trying to share that same reflection of Jesus in his home.

"I'm sensitive to the supernatural, and I gotta tell ya they was angels that came up in that joint last night. I slept like a baby!"

Michael was amazed by what had happened in his apartment with his roommate, but he was even more amazed at how Jesus had changed his own life since he had decided to follow Him.

"Jesus changes everything, don't he, P.S.?"

"Yes, He does, Michael. Yes, He does!"

This life change in Michael was epic, and we were blessed to have a front-row seat watching him become more and more like Jesus.

Still, the road ahead of Michael wouldn't be easy.

He would be tested.

He would encounter more struggle, more frustration, more spiritual battle, and his greatest nemesis wouldn't be a hotheaded roommate but, of all people, a street preacher.

12

Miracles

George was one of the first faces we used to see every morning at Cadence. He would walk through the door with a chipper "Good morning!"

George was Chattanooga's shoe shiner. If you wanted to see him light up, just ask him about shining shoes. He was always proud of his work. Word on the street was that he was a shoe shiner in the movie *42*, the Jackie Robinson story that was partially filmed in Chattanooga.

George always tried to stretch every penny he had. He always smelled like aftershave, and he always brought a bit of shine to the room when he walked through the door.

Most mornings, he would show me something that I just had to see—a hat someone gave him, a jacket he picked up at the community kitchen, or a new-to-him pair of old boots that someone had given him.

One morning, it was a bottle of medicine. He brought the bottle up to the counter and showed it to me as if he had just won a first-prize trophy. His excitement was more gratitude than it was any sort of pride. George was grateful to finally have a prescription he needed to help keep food down. George had stomach cancer and had been living with it for quite a while. He was truly optimistic that things were going to turn around for him. He'd always been a thin-framed man, but recently he had seemed more frail than usual, and now it all made sense. He was literally being eaten alive by cancer.

"How ya doin', George?"

"Oh, I'll be all right now! Got me some medicine to help me keep my food down!"

"Is your cancer worse?" I asked him.

"Yeah, but I'll be all right." Tears puddled in his fear-filled eyes.

"What can I do for you, George?"

"You gotta biscuit I can eat? I'm hungry, and this medicine is gonna help me keep it down now!"

His weak, fearful eyes suddenly seemed to glimmer with hope and anticipation. We heated up an English muffin sandwich for him, and while it was heating, we prayed together.

I shared George's situation with our church family and a few friends who I knew would pray for him. The number of people who replied saying they would pray and who later asked about him—and frequently—was remarkable. I told him.

"George, you wouldn't believe the folks that are praying for you to get better."

Those familiar tears trickled down his cheeks as he asked, "For me? They prayin' for me?"

"Yes, sir!"

He just shook his head and walked away to put a little cream and sugar his half-filled cup of coffee. He never wanted a full cup.

Early on at Cadence, we created a Pay It Forward system, where customers could pay two dollars for a cup of coffee for someone else. It wasn't necessarily intended for the homeless, but they did seem to be the customers who asked for a Pay It Forward most often. We've all been in a situation where we've stepped up to the counter to pay for something that we've ordered, only to discover that we left our wallet or any form of payment at home or in the car. We saw the Pay It Forward plan as a win-win for everyone and anyone.

When a customer buys a Pay It Forward, we encourage them to write a few kind words on the back of the Pay It Forward card. When another customer needs a Pay It Forward, we give them a twelve-ounce cup of coffee and the card with the note written on the back.

He could have had a full cup of coffee every time he asked for a Pay It Forward, but George only ever asked for half a cup. Initially, I thought he only wanted half, or maybe his stomach couldn't handle a full cup of coffee, but later I realized his reasoning in asking for half a cup was twofold. He didn't want to take too much; he knew he wasn't paying, and he didn't want to take advantage of someone else's kindness. Secondly, he loved getting the note on the Pay It Forward. I'm not sure he could read all that well, but he certainly tried. He would leave an empty cup, but he always took his note with him.

Over time, the medicine worked, and George was able to eat again. A friend brought a huge supply of groceries to Cadence just for

George. When George came in, I showed him the bags of groceries, and he was blown away, like a kid at Christmas.

This friend had thought of everything, and George was speechless with gratitude. One by one, he showed me each item they brought to him. "Looky here! That'll be good to eat!"

George traveled on foot downtown, and the food that had been delivered for him was way too much for him to carry around all over town. He asked if we could keep the stash at Cadence, and he would come back throughout the week and get a little at a time.

"Church folk, they good folk, ain't they?" he asked.

"They are, George. These folks love Jesus, George, and Jesus loves you. They love who He loves. That means they love you!"

He shook his head. "The Lord is good to me!"

It was quite some time later that George came bouncing into Cadence—as usual, the first customer of the day. He was smiling from ear to ear.

"Cancer-free!" he shouted.

My jaw dropped to the counter. "Seriously? Totally cancer-free?"

"Sho nuf," he bragged. "The good Lord done healed ole George. I'm cancer-free I tell ya."

He knew exactly when it happened too. One morning sitting at the table in the back left corner of our café side, George was sipping on his half cup of coffee. He recounted a moment when a thin streak of light came right in through the front door of the café. He said that it ran along the floor and right up to his table, encircled the edge of the table, and hit his hands. He said he felt heat in his hands that went right through his whole body, and he knew something had happened. That was the moment when he knew that Jesus walked right up to his table and healed him.

He was so excited, and we were too.

George's miracle was a big miracle to him. Watching this man practically come back to life was a sight to behold. People loved George, and so many folks stepped up to care for him so well. He drew a check every month, but during his sickness, you could tell things got harder for him, and without a great deal of solicitation, people stepped up and gave him boxes and boxes of food.

We laughed about him gaining weight and how he still looked like an old skeleton sometimes.

"We'll fix that," he said.

"I gotta big ole bag, heavy bag, of Ensure waitin' fa me down the street! It's too heavy fa me to carry all over town, so I'm goin out ta Walmart get me a new warm coat with this here gift card somebody gave me. Then I'm goin' down er en get 'em Ensure cans!"

He was a man with a plan, "blessed and highly favored" in his words.

A real-life miracle right in front of our eyes.

On the other side of the table, where we were all talking, sat Tim. Tim was another miracle, one in the making. He had recently come off the streets. He, too, had been so excited. He sat there with us as we listened to George go on and on about how he was going to get all his weight back on. It was a fun conversation really. Lighthearted. We laughed a lot. George soon left, and I turned to Tim and asked him how he had been feeling. He'd had some health issues lately. "Oh, I'm going to be fine, just fine," he said. He was on heart medicine now, and his doctor was taking good care of him.

He told me that the last two times he had been to see his doctor, he was down twenty pounds. He had lost nearly forty pounds in two months.

"Why have you lost forty pounds in two months, Tim? That's not healthy."

"I know," he responded, "but like I told my doctor, it's the best I could do."

"What do you mean it's the best you can do?" I asked.

Tim had already experienced the miraculous in his life, but he still needed a few more miracles—big ones.

13

Band-Aids

"I'm off the streets; that's all that matters."

A few months earlier, Tim was sitting on a park bench next to the Tivoli Theater when Jacob, our general manager, came walking by. Tim asked him for a cigarette. Jacob didn't have one, but he did invite him to go up the street to Cadence for a cup of coffee. It would be some time before Tim would walk through the doors of the café for that first cup of coffee. In the short time Jacob sat with Tim on that park bench, they talked about life, but before he left, Jacob offered to pray with him. It wasn't a complicated prayer but one that God would answer right in front of all our eyes.

A few days later when Tim walked into Cadence for his first Pay It Forward, he was a bit weirded out.

"I couldn't figure out why everyone was being so nice to me. They didn't know me, but if they did, I was sure they wouldn't be nice to me for long."

Tim had quite the past. Many dark days checkered the earlier years of his life. There were places where Tim left quite a bit of scorched earth behind him. Eventually, he started coming to church on Sunday mornings, and each week, he was welcomed, hugged, and made to feel like family by someone new. Eventually, he got a job at the Tivoli, cleaning up after shows at the theater. It wasn't great, but it was a job, and Tim was grateful. It wasn't the easiest job for him either. The only pair of shoes Tim owned was a heavy pair of black boots that were too small for his swollen feet and ankles, and one Sunday, I noticed him rubbing his legs and feet, and I could tell he was in pain.

"You good, man?"

"Yeah, but these boots are killing me. I stand on my feet for hours at my job, and by the end of the shift, I feel like my feet are going to bust right out of my boots."

It came time for worship to start and then for me to share the sermon for that day. Honestly, I don't remember what I talked about that Sunday. I doubt anyone remembers, because what happened in the last five minutes of our gathering was more powerful than anything I could have ever preached.

"We have a new friend who started a new job recently. His only pair of shoes are some heavy boots, and they are making it really hard to do his job. He's needing a pair of ten-and-a-half shoes. If anyone has a pair they could bring to him, he would be happy to have them for work this week."

Without any warning, or even a split second to process what was happening, Bruce walked straight over to Tim with a pair of sneakers—size 10 1/2. Bruce walked back across the room to his seat, in his sock feet. Tim was speechless. I was too.

This.

This is the very thing I had hoped and prayed for when we moved to town years earlier to plant this church in this city. This was the ministry of Jesus, and Tim was experiencing this ministry in the person of Bruce and Bruce's shoes. Best of all, others were following the example of Jesus. I wasn't the only one seeing and experiencing Jesus from behind the bar, outside the four walls of the church. Others were too—Jacob sitting on a park bench to encourage and pray for a random stranger, Bruce offering his shoes right then and there off his feet. This and so many other selfless acts among our staff and church family were exactly what Jesus would do if He were presently visibly living among us.

Tim kept his job and saved enough money to be able to move into his own apartment. Life for him was as it should be—off the streets, a job, basic needs provided. Or so we assumed.

Tim sat at a table and listened to George talk about all the food he had been given and how blessed he was, and he smiled a smile of gratitude on George's behalf. He was truly happy to celebrate with someone else who had also seen hard days, now experiencing a better life. Tim was blessed to have a bed to sleep in and saw no reason to complain to anyone. Life for him was so much better now than it ever had been before.

Problem was Tim had no food in his apartment at all—nothing. He spent all the resources he had saved to get into a place to live, sacrificing what he needed to make sure he was off the streets, even if it meant food. When I learned that he didn't have the first bite of food in his house, we rallied the troops. In no time, the

RiverChurch community stepped up around Tim to make sure he had a pantry full of food. Collectively, we determined that this would never happen again. We realized helping Tim would require more than just a one-time act of benevolence. A long road of recovery from poverty lay ahead, and we were going to walk it with him, if he would let us.

Chattanooga has been called the most Benevolent City in the United States. That's a complimentary moniker for our small southern city. I believe it. Folks around here seem to love helping others less fortunate. But like anyone with a heart to help, sometimes we tend to help with Band-Aids and go missing for the convalescent care. Sometimes we can help, when really we're not helping but hurting.

In 2009, a couple of professors from Covenant College, up on Lookout Mountain, wrote a book called *When Helping Hurts; Alleviating Poverty without Hurting the Poor ... and Yourself.* Steve Corbett and Brian Fikkert assert that alleviating poverty involves more than just providing material needs for those who lack, but that it also means helping people move toward a meaningful relationship with God, themselves, others, and all of creation. In other words, helping people in poverty doesn't stop with handing out free food. If we truly intend to help, we should prepare to do more than just apply a Band-Aid; we must prepare for a long road ahead.

Tim's situation opened our eyes to a stark reality that can be found in any city where poverty exists. Most of us can walk into our kitchen, open the refrigerator, and take out something to eat any time we want. We walk to our pantry, stand there, and look for the right snack to ease our late-night cravings. Meanwhile, on the other side of town, someone just like Tim is in their apartment with a microwave and a cooler that someone gave them, but they have no food to heat in that microwave or keep cool in that cooler. Tim didn't just need help getting into an apartment, furnishing it with a few appliances and his first round of groceries. He needed folks to lock arms with him, to walk with him, to check in on him regularly, and to make sure he continued to have food to eat.

We learned that there is another side to homelessness and poverty. Some people are stuck in dire straits simply because they don't have someone to help them get out and stay out. On the streets, you can find someone giving out a free meal every day of the week and multiple times each day. At least that's the case here in Chattanooga. When a person comes off the streets, they may or may not have access to resources to help with their basic needs. We have an area food bank and countless other nonprofits who are willing to help with basic needs, but some folks like Tim struggle to find transportation to get to these places to receive the help they so desperately need. Right here in our city, and most likely in yours, there are kids who sleep on floors who have no beds. Kitchens without refrigeration or stoves to prepare food, or empty pantries with no food to prepare if they do have those basic amenities. In your city, there are families that choose not to turn on lighs or heat, because they can't afford the electric bill.

God taught us a huge lesson through Tim. We aren't meant to help others so we can lay our heads on our comfortable pillows at night and feel better about ourselves. If we want to truly help people stop the bleeding from a painful life of poverty, we must do more than just apply Band-Aids. Helping requires commitment, not just a one-and-done experience.

Now that can seem intimidating and might scare some people away. In fact, one regret Corbett and Fikkert shared after writing their book was that some people seemed to stop helping all together. I know this adage is a bit out of context, but "it takes a village." At least it did for Tim. Derek and Janet, Mark and Darlene, Bruce and Rita, Jacob, another Tim, and so many in our church family invaded his life, refusing to let him go hungry, but more than that, refusing to let him live life on his own. Tim needed more than a Band-Aid; he needed healing hands to help him, to walk with him and hold his hands, even in the darkest and loneliest of times, and that's just what we did.

14

OUTLAW

One afternoon on my way home from Cadence, I had the strange urge to listen to the radio. Typically, my driving home soundtrack comes from Spotify or a podcast, but this day I had the urge to listen to something from the FM airwaves. It's a habit that drives my wife crazy, but sometimes I just like to hit the scan button and let the radio roll through area radio stations for five-second windows so I can hear what they're playing. If something catches my attention, I stop the scan and take a listen. That's what happened when I scanned right to an old country classic that I had never heard before.

Now understand, I'm no country music connoisseur, but occasionally, I like to hear a little Johnny Cash, Dolly Parton, Reba, or Brad Paisley. This was a slow, twangy ballad called "Outlaw's Prayer" by Johnny Paycheck. He doesn't even sing in this song; it's sort of a mashup of spoken word meets honky-tonk narrative. Paycheck tells of a time when he walked up to a church and started to go in, but someone met him at the door and told him he couldn't come in because of the way he was dressed.

It's a scathing little dirge really. Paycheck gives a solid gut punch to highbrow church folks, and honestly, I was a little put out by it. It felt sensational, unbelievable.

I know I tend to be naive, and I had heard of situations like this before, but I struggle to believe that any real Christians would ever turn someone away from the doors of a church, for any reason. It does make a great little ballad for an old country music singer, accompanied by a steel and a base guitar in a honky-tonk somewhere. Still, I was doubtful.

Later that evening, I got a call from Tim. He had been invited to a wedding and didn't have anything to wear. So, he was asking if I knew where he could get a cheap sports jacket.

"What size do you wear? I'll ask around."

He guessed at a size and then seemed to take a sentimental tone.

"I know I don't say it much, but I'm truly thankful for you, Cadence, and RiverChurch, because there was a time when I wasn't allowed to enter a church building."

"Really? What do you mean?"

"Yep," he replied.

Then he asked me an ironic question that left me in a small state of shock.

"You ever heard that song 'The Outlaw's Prayer'?"

I was silent.

"Uh … yeah … I literally heard it for the first time today and actually thought it was a far-fetched way to make Christians look bad!"

"Nope," he said. "That kind of stuff happens. Happened to me, and I never thought I'd ever go back to another church again."

He did, and I'm so thankful he didn't just come to church; he became family.

Tim had a record. He had served time for a lot of bad choices he had made in his younger years. He was a dark-skinned fellow with jet-black hair that in his prime was very popular among the ladies. He fathered a lot of kids, none of whom talked to him now. He had done too much, broken too many hearts, and after prison found himself on the streets. We watched him move from a park bench to his own place, and while his health was deteriorating from a hard life lived, we could see new life in this old outlaw.

Tim went public with his faith one Father's Day. We typically like to go down to the Tennessee River for baptisms, but he was having an increasingly hard time walking, so we filled our cattle trough at Cadence, and we baptized him right there that Sunday morning. He was a new man. He didn't look like the same Tim who asked Jacob for a cigarette a year or so earlier.

He wanted a haircut and to clean up before his baptism, so I took him to my buddy Laith, who gave him the best shave and cut he had ever had. His handsome features seemed to rise to the surface, and he looked good, really good. But nothing could compare to the beauty that was on his face the morning we took him into the waters of baptism. This man had changed; it was real change. Not because of a cup of coffee, or an apartment, or a truck load of groceries, or a sports coat, or a group of church folks who simply had learned to love and live like Jesus. No, those were all just tools that Jesus Himself had used to bring this outlaw into the family of faith, and that Father's Day, we celebrated his new life as family.

Tim's health began to fail quickly. He was suffering from congestive heart failure, and the doctor told him that there was nothing else they could do for him. We painfully watched as Tim was essentially smothering to death every day with his heart condition. The last Sunday he was at church, Tim was in a wheelchair, his voice was weak, and his entire body was swollen with fluid. His skin looked gray, and we all had a sense that this would be one of the last times we would see him. I legitimately feared that Tim would die alone at home with only his dog, Patch, by his side. But after our gathering that day, Mark and Darlene opened their home and invited Tim to come stay with them. Darlene works in health care, so she knew how to offer him the best possible care even as his health continued to deteriorate.

Later that week, I went to their house, and as I walked into their living room, directly in front of the door was a hospital bed, with Tim lying in it, breathing shallow and laboriously.

I wish you could have seen the small army of people who surrounded Tim that week. We had people working tirelessly to help him get his affairs in order, reaching out to his kids, sitting with him around the clock, reading scripture to him, praying with him, and singing over him. It was nothing short of awe-inspiring. Tim stayed with Mark and Darlene for nearly a week, and in that time, thanks to Darlene's bulldog tenacity, we were able to locate an assisted-living facility that offered hospice care to Tim. The facility was a far distance from his apartment or his old life downtown and from Cadence as well, but it did just happen to be down the road from where Mick, another RiverChurch family member, lived. Mick went to see Tim regularly and was able to keep the rest of our church family informed of the ever-fluctuating condition of his health.

To our surprise and great joy, Tim began to improve. The nurses were able to regulate his medications and ensure that he was taking everything he needed. Turns out Tim was a typical old bachelor who wasn't very good at staying on top of his meds, but here in assisted living, his medicine came to him every day like clockwork, and he was turning the corner.

Tim improved so much that he was able to move from the hospice unit to a more independent assisted-living unit of the same facility. Mick would take him out for ice cream from time to time, allowing him to enjoy the simple things in life just a little bit longer.

Tim became quite the ladies' man in the assisted-living facility. We had genuinely seen life change in him, but even the best of folks struggle with aspects of their past after they've decided to follow Jesus. Tim became somewhat of a Casanova in the assisted-living facility, capturing the hearts of ladies and then breaking them to the point that we got a phone call from one of the nurses asking us to have a conversation with him. I think Derrick was the lucky one who had to tell Tim to "act his age." Hopefully, the conversation was effective; we never heard anything else from the nurses about Tim's soap opera life. But we could tell that life on the inside was a struggle for this old outlaw who had lived behind a set of bars; this form of institutional living felt all too familiar. Eventually, Tim decided to make a run for it. Apparently, he found a lady friend, and they lived together until he had to go back into assisted living again.

From the very beginning, we understood that God had brought this outlaw to us and had called us to take him in. To love him. To do life with him no longer an as outlaw but as a member of a real family.

15

Lifeline

It was a Tuesday morning in March when Matthew came stumbling through the doors of Cadence. He didn't look well. He was shivering and sweating at the same time. He sat on our front couch for a few minutes and then came up to the counter and asked for a bottle of apple juice. He went back to the couch and sat down with his juice. Every few minutes, he stood back up and limped his way to the restroom. This was his practice for several hours throughout the entire day.

Hours before, he had been released from the city jail, which was located a block behind the café. The evening before, Matthew had found himself in a domestic dispute with his parents. Things escalated to the point that his parents called the police, he went to jail for the night, and now he was simply trying to figure out what to do next.

His current possessions included the black pants and white T-shirt he was wearing, a single pair of shoes, a cell phone, and his wallet. He seemed to regularly take inventory of himself to make sure he wasn't separated from any of his personal effects.

Gina was our cashier on shift that day. She'd been a RiverChurch family member from day one. Gina also believed in the power of prayer and the importance of praying on the spot. She noticed that things weren't all right with Matthew, so she walked over to the couch where he was sitting and asked if she could pray for him. He politely refused her offer and continued his routine trek back and forth to the restroom.

Eventually, I walked over to him and sat with him and asked if everything was OK. That's when he told me about the events of the evening before. To say he was frustrated was an understatement. He had tried and tried to reach his parents, but they weren't taking his calls. He felt they were being paranoid and excessive in their response to the argument from the night before.

"Man, you don't look well. Do you need to go to the hospital?" I asked.

"No," he flatly refused.

I pressed a little further to discover that Matthew was on some significant pain medication. He had sustained a gun-related injury a little more than a year before that had left him crippled on one side and now heavily dependent on pain meds. He assured me that if he could just get in touch with his dad, he would ask his dad to get him his meds, and he would be right as rain. But dad wasn't answering the phone.

I went back to make a few drinks, checking on him periodically.

After lunch, a small group of fifth graders visiting Chattanooga from South Carolina were brought into Cadence by their teacher, who presumably needed a dose of caffeine to carry her through the afternoon. While the teacher ordered, the kids sat on a bench against the wall just a few feet from where Matthew was sitting, slumped over on the couch, shivering and shuffling back and forth. Realizing that her students were completely captivated by what was happening to this guy, the teacher herded her students to our gathering room side while they waited for her latte to be made. Once she had them settled in the other room, she walked up to me and inquired about Matthew.

"Is he OK?" she asked.

"No, he's not, but he's refusing to see a doctor, and we're really concerned about him."

"I'm actually a registered nurse. Would you care if I went and talked to him?"

"Please!" I begged her.

She carefully walked over to Matthew and introduced herself to him.

"Hi there! My name is Sarah. What's yours?"

"Matthew."

"Matthew, are you OK?" she asked as she carefully put her hand on his arm.

He didn't even seem to notice this stranger touching him. He explained that he would be fine. He had medicine at home, and he just needed to get to it. They talked for a few more minutes, and then she echoed our pleas for him to go seek medical help.

"Matthew, you're actually very sick right now. I've been monitoring your pulse as we've been talking." Her hands had been resting on his wrist to feel his pulse.

"Your pulse is very slow, and it seems to have been getting slower as we've been talking. I'm concerned that you may be experiencing some serious withdrawal effects from your medication, and I think you could be in a dangerous place right now. I really think you should go to the emergency room."

Still, he resisted.

"OK, then, well … I'm also a follower of Jesus, and I don't believe it's by chance that I walked in here today with my fifth graders. I'm going to pray for you now."

Matthew had no opportunity to refuse this time. She just started praying. Quietly. Simply.

"In Jesus's name, amen."

She walked over to me afterward with a look of concern yet a peaceful smile on her face.

"I'm glad we came in here today. He was why I was supposed to bring my class. He needs to see a doctor, but if he doesn't, I just prayed that he would be restored to health."

We thanked her for coming, and as she left, we were convinced that God had indeed brought her in that day.

After Sarah left, I went back over to Matthew to reason with him again.

"Matthew, we want to help you, but you have to let us help you. Can we take you to the hospital?" Jacob had come in by this time for the closing shift, and we were trying to reason with Matthew together.

"I don't want to go to the hospital. There may be police there, and I don't want to be around any cops."

Matthew was avoiding police officers because of some negative interactions he had experienced with them in recent months. Rightfully or wrongfully, he didn't trust them and didn't want to even risk being around them. He was convinced he would run into police at the emergency room. I didn't press him for more information but continued to pray for direction as to how to help him.

A few minutes later, I asked Matthew if he thought his dad would take my phone call if I called from a number other than his. He thought he would, so I called from my own phone.

Matthew's dad didn't answer initially, so I left a voice mail explaining Matthew's condition and asked him to give me a call as soon as he could. Not even half an hour went by before my phone rang.

I could tell he was skeptical at first of who I was. I explained that I owned the coffee shop where his son was sitting at that moment. I also explained that I was a pastor and really wanted to do what I could to help. This softened his posture a little. He agreed to meet me privately, not with Matthew. Matthew had done too much damage to their relationship not just the night before but also in recent months, and they would not subject themselves to his anger any longer. We agreed to meet later that evening to get his medicine, his cane, and a change of clothes. When I hung up the phone, I told Matthew the plan, but I intentionally complicated things for him a bit.

"I'll get you your things, Matthew, but only after you've seen a doctor." He wasn't happy with me.

"I can't just leave you out there hoping you're going to be OK. You have to go to the emergency room if you want your things."

He didn't cave, not for a while at least.

It had to be no more than thirty minutes later that, of all people, the chief of police walked in for an afternoon cup of coffee. Suddenly Matthew was even more uncomfortable than he had already been.

"He's safe, Matthew. We know him!"

The chief was a friend of Cadence. We explained what was happening and that we really wanted to see Matthew get medical attention.

"Hey, man," the chief said.

"I don't know you, and you don't know me, but these guys are throwing you a lifeline. If I were you, I would take it. Otherwise, this day could end very poorly for you. Take the help, man."

I'm not sure if Matthew was tired of protesting or he simply didn't want to have any further conversation with the man in blue, but suddenly he agreed to go to the emergency room.

We didn't give him much time to change his mind. Within minutes, we pulled a car up to the front door, and we drove him straight to the closest hospital. I told him that I would go meet his dad and be back at the hospital later with his things and help him get settled for the night.

It was a few hours later that I met Matthew's dad in a parking lot in another part of town. Dean got out of his van and met me with his son's cane and a small backpack.

"How is he?" Dean asked with a noticeably worried look on his face.

"I think he's going to be OK now."

I explained our plan and that I would be seeing him shortly.

"We love him, we really do, but we can't keep living like this."

Dean went on to explain quite a lot of personal and family details surrounding their relationship with Matthew. It was as if he immediately trusted me without even knowing me. The past few months, after the gun accident, had practically destroyed Matthew personally and his relationship with those closest to him. They were at the end of their rope and obviously had nothing left to give. I understood that.

"I don't know how much we can help him, but it's obvious to me that God brought him to us today, so we're going to do whatever we can."

Reminded of the words of the police chief earlier, I assured Matthew's dad by saying, "We're throwing him a lifeline; hopefully he will grab on and let us help."

"When you see him again," his dad said as he was getting in his car, "tell him …"—his voice cracked a little—"tell him we love him."

And so the journey with Matthew—and his family—began.

16

TABLE IN THE CORNER

He couldn't go home. He had all but destroyed the relationship he had with his family. They simply couldn't take it anymore. He had pushed them all away. Now he was alone.

I went with my friend Alex to pick Matthew up from the emergency room, and we took him to a weekly stay hotel that we had booked for him.

"Where are we going?"

The emergency room doctor had given him some liquids and some medicine to level him out a bit. He had improved significantly.

"We rented you a room to stay in for the week, man. We want to help you. We don't know exactly what that will look like, but we're willing."

By now, we had well learned the importance of walking the long road if necessary. This would certainly be no one-and-done type of help.

"I have money; I'll pay you back. Wait, why are you doing this? You don't have to do this! I can pay you back." All of this was way too much for him to process.

"Come back to Cadence tomorrow, and we can talk about all of that. For tonight, get some rest."

We checked him into his hotel. He still couldn't put all the pieces together as to why we were helping him. He shook his head as he said, "Good night," and walked toward his room.

Matthew came to Cadence later the next morning. He was a different man. You could tell a night of sleep was what he needed.

Day after day for nearly six months, he would come into the shop and just hang out at the table in the corner. He loved it there. He said he felt safe, felt something different. He trusted us. During those six months, I got to know his parents. Salt of the earth kind of people. They truly loved Matthew, but they were determined to not let things go back to the dark place they had been before. What Matthew needed the most in this season was tough love, and that's the kind of love they were prepared to show him.

The day he came into Cadence after that overnight stay in jail, Matthew had missed an appointment with a probation officer. That missed appointment landed him in jail for thirty days not long after he started to come to Cadence on a regular basis. Until that point, I had never been inside a jail. The county jail was a couple of blocks away from Cadence. I often thought about the people inside behind the bars, as I walked into work. Now I personally knew someone on the inside.

The first time I went to see him, I waited, and he never showed. His floor had been put on lockdown because of some unruly inmates, so we never got to talk. I scheduled another visit sometime later and went to see him. He looked tired, dejected, and hopeless. Like Matthew, the people behind those bars were all in there for a reason. Right or wrong, good or bad. Their life had taken a turn that had led them to this place. Part of me wanted to cry. The sense of hopelessness in that place made me feel nauseous as I talked to him through a telephone receiver, separated by a glass window.

Eventually, Matthew served his thirty days, and he was released. By this time, numerous conversations had transpired between Matthew's parents and me. With a great deal of reservation, they decided to let him come back home. Their reunion was pleasant, hugs and smiles, but short-lived.

Matthew and I stayed in communication while he lived with his parents. From time to time, they would get into arguments, and his dad would call me, asking me to pray or talk to him. Matthew had an addiction to alcohol. When he drank heavily, the alcohol and the prescription medications created a dangerous cocktail of hostility and conflict.

One day, Dean called me while Matthew was raging.

"Shannon! Please pray for us. He's yelling and screaming and saying mean things, and we just don't know what to do."

That phone call lasted for a while, and there was a follow-up conversation the next day. Matthew ultimately agreed to work harder on his relationship with his parents but not for long. Another eruption took place a few weeks later, and for Dean and Donna, this was the last straw.

They didn't have him arrested; they just had him removed from the house. Enough was enough. So one Sunday while they were gone, a police officer showed up at their house and instructed Matthew to get his things, that his parents had called and asked that they would remove him from the home. He was taken by surprise but he was complicit. Later that evening, he called me to tell me what had happened. He was back at the hotel where we had originally put him up the first time.

He was mad at his parents, and while he actively looked for a more permanent place to stay, Matthew resumed his daily visits to Cadence. He was on disability because of the permanent injury to his leg. His disability kept him from working a full-time job, so he would volunteer at the shop. Some days, he would stamp cup sleeves or sweep the floors. On occasion, he helped us with some baking. He had been a professional chef back in the day. But lots of heartache, overdependence on pain meds, and alcohol abuse had pretty much stolen his life from him. He saw himself as a victim. Maybe he was. From Matthew's point of view though, everyone else had the problems. He acknowledged he had his own, but they had bigger issues, and many of our conversations consisted of him railing against all the people who had done him wrong.

One day, I sat down with Matthew at the table in the corner, and we had a long, honest conversation about faith.

"Shannon, I know you believe all of this Jesus stuff. I used to too. But I don't anymore."

Dean had told me that when Matthew was a kid, he would find his sermon notes from back in the day when he was an army chaplain. He would take Dean's notes to his room and preach the same sermon that his dad preached. Somewhere along the way, Matthew stopped believing.

I answered his question as best I could, telling him why I believed all of this "Jesus stuff." I told him how I had come to faith as a small child and had lived my entire life following Christ on some level. I told him how Jesus had proven Himself to be real to me time and time again. I told him after all of the years I had been alive and all that I had seen, I simply could not *not* believe all of this Jesus stuff.

He laughed, not in a mocking way but more like a "that's ironic" kind of way.

"You sound just like Sam."

Sam was a guy Matthew met in jail during his thirty days. Sam had recently made a decision to follow Christ and had plenty of time to share his story with Matthew behind the bars of the city jail. Sam's grandparents were also part of our RiverChurch family. Every Sunday after our gathering, they would drive around the jail or to the top floor of the parking garage next to Cadence that sat directly beside the jail. The jail had windows, so Sam's grandparents would wave as they circled the jail in hopes that Sam would look out any one of those windows to see them.

Now anyone would be extremely hard-pressed to convince me that Matthew's stumbling into Cadence six months before, the journey we had walked together, the fact that Matthew had met Sam in jail, and Sam's connection back to RiverChurch—that all of this was just coincidence.

"Matthew, all of these random things only further convince me that God is real, and He's trying to get your attention."

Matthew had often told me about the day that he walked down Seventh Street away from the city jail. On one side of the street was a Chinese restaurant with a beer sign flashing in the window. On the other side was a coffee shop. He thought it was odd that he liked beer and didn't like coffee and yet he chose to come into the coffee shop.

"That wasn't coincidence. God brought you here. He wanted you to have a real encounter with Jesus, right here, Matthew. For so long, the enemy of your soul has tried to destroy you, but God brought you here to us, to find Jesus."

The only thing hiding Matthew's tears were the dark sunglasses he was wearing, but even they couldn't hide his emotion. He put his head down on the table and wept. Once again, this table in the corner had become a sacred space, like it was for George when he was healed from cancer, and like it was for Michael the night he came in with a heart full of hate. Now here sat Matthew. I could see the tenderness of Jesus melting his hardened heart. He didn't say anything; he just cried. But I just knew that God was softening Matthew's heart. What I didn't know was that this would be our very last conversation, sitting there at the table in the corner.

17

Unknown

He came into Cadence that afternoon in typical fashion. Regardless of the kind of day he was having, Michael always seemed to dramatically blow into the café like a loud and frazzled whirlwind. If it was a good day, he would fling the door open, stand squarely at the threshold, and greet everyone inside with a Marvin Gaye kind of greeting. "What's goin' onnnnnn, people?"

This wasn't that kind of day.

The door flew open, and he bulldozed right inside, straight to the bar, past any other customer in line. His head was tilted down, and his eyes were intensely set on me as he walked in my direction.

"We need to talk," he said, pointing his finger at me.

I recognized that tone, that look, that finger. It's the kind my wife gives me when I forget to put the toilet seat down in the middle of the night, or after I've unknowingly said something embarrassing in my sermon on Sunday morning (which happens a lot). In moments like that, the only thing I can think to do is duck, hide, or run. But I knew I hadn't done anything to get in trouble with Michael; I hadn't seen him in a long time. So I just stood there and braced myself for whatever he was about to unleash, while casting an apologetic look to the unsuspecting customers standing nearby.

Michael came in to give me a fully detailed report of a terse exchange he'd had with a street preacher who stood at the end of our block on the corner of Market and Seventh. Michael and Street Preacher seemed to have a mutual and ongoing dislike for each other. Now I'm not sure what Michael ever specifically said to Street Preacher, but I do know Michael, and I'm sure he offered his fair share of provoking banter. Still, I couldn't imagine him saying anything that would warrant the kind of castigation and ridicule that Street Preacher always seemed to throw Michael's way.

Street Preacher didn't know Michael. He seemed only to engage with him from a place of assumption and prejudice. He never really had a real, meaningful, or intentional conversation with him. He never tried to learn anything about Michael's life. He only seemed to be convinced of where Michael would spend eternity, and he never missed an opportunity to tell him. Over time and after countless fruitless conversations, Michael had learned to let it roll off his back—but not today. No, on this particular day, it was way too much for Michael to simply let it roll off.

On his way up the street to Cadence, Street Preacher said something to Michael about how he needed to get into church, or he was going to hell. Michael quickly and proudly reported to Street Preacher, "I *do* go to church! Right up the road there at Cadence Coffee."

Like so many times before, Street Preacher seemed to take a big gulp from an invisible cup of ignorance and said, "I know about that place. That ain't no church." He proceeded to use some colorful language to describe Cadence and RiverChurch.

For the record, Street Preacher has never darkened the door of Cadence or RiverChurch. He and I have never had a conversation at all. I've passed him on the streets countless times, and honestly, I've never engaged him either. His tone was always robotic, as was his posture. He would just stand on the street corner quoting scripture of fire and damnation, with no emotion, never seeming to even blink. I never saw the slightest characteristic of Jesus. Never an invitation to passersby to "come let us reason together." I often found myself embarrassed that this man was poorly representing Jesus, and honestly, right or wrong, I felt like engaging him would simply be a waste of both of our times.

How he knew anything about Cadence or RiverChurch was beyond me.

"Somebody better hold me back," Michael said, shaking his head and wiping the sweat from his brow, "cuz I wanna go back down there and give him a good ole ..." He balled up his fist and pumped it toward my face.

Further proof of life change was demonstrated in Michael's wise choice not to react. Instead, he just beelined his way to Cadence and busted through the door.

"Ya'll gonna need to pray for me, 'cause that dude done gone and made me mad—real mad."

He was. His chin was pulled in tightly, more sweat was dripping from his face, and his eyebrows were pinched tightly together.

I wasn't really bothered by Street Preacher's insults. This man seemed to live in a cloud of unknown. He didn't know Michael, he didn't know us, and he certainly didn't know how to effectively reach the masses with the true Gospel of Jesus. While I was disappointed in what he had said to Michael, I certainly wasn't bothered by him. Not nearly as bothered as Michael.

We prayed with Michael and asked God to settle his heart and mind. We told him that Jesus Himself had religious folks say bad things about Him and His disciples, and how He said we were blessed when that kind of thing happened to us. I even tried to lighten Michael's mood with a little humor.

"That's awesome!" I said with a huge smile on my face.

"What?" Michael looked at me with great skepticism.

"I've certainly been called plenty of names before, and most of them were far worse than what that fella called us. I think our reputation in town may be improving!"

Michael's tense expression crumbled to a wide smile, and he chuckled a little, still not quite ready to let go of his anger. Kevin, a midday regular at Cadence and RiverChurch family member, happened to be standing around throughout this entire conversation. He encouraged Michael at some point, if not that day, to take Street Preacher a cup of coffee. To just walk up to him and hand him a cup and then walk away. We all daydreamed for a minute or two what his reaction to Michael's act of kindness might do to him. He didn't take Street Preacher coffee that day but indicated he would, eventually. He didn't stay mad for long either. In fact, he left Cadence that afternoon laughing his long, rapid-fire kind of cackle. He threw out a few high fives to some customers standing in line and shouted from the door, "Keep it real, ya'll."

I'd love to tie this story up with a nice bow and a happy ending, but truthfully, we never knew what happened.

Did Michael talk to Street Preacher again?

Did he ever take him that cup of coffee?

I don't know. In fact, I haven't seen Michael since that conversation. I've certainly looked for him, prayed for him, asked God if he was OK, to give me some sort of something to know where he is and that he is OK. You know what I've found out about Michael? Nothing. Simply left with the unknown.

This isn't an isolated instance of unknown though. We experience the unknown a lot and often with the people we meet through Cadence. That's especially true with people in the homeless community or folks without the means to communicate with us where they are or what has happened to them.

Sometimes our regular customers will move away and will tell us they're leaving. But there are plenty of times when we notice that we haven't seen a particular customer in a while, and we're left with unknowns. What happened? Where did they go? Are they OK? Sometimes I'll see folks who used to be regulars walking around town with a cup from another coffee shop in their hands. If we see each other, they might look at me a little sheepishly, as if they expect me to be mad. I'm not. I get it. It's a little funny. I drink coffee from other coffee shops in town too.

Over the span of our years of operation, we've literally seen thousands of people walk through our doors. Some of them come and go, and we never really make much of a connection with them. But there are others, plenty of others, with whom we've built some sort of camaraderie, and our paths of life converge for a season, and then we go our separate ways.

It's never easy. But it's especially hard when you've invested in a person's life, and suddenly they're gone, vanished into the unknown.

What happened to them?
Where did they go?
Where are they now?

Tim left us with unknowns.

I received the following text in December 2020 from a RiverChurch family member: "I found out recently that Tim died in July. His widow (the lady who broke him out of the nursing home was how she identified herself) found my name in his phone and called me to tell me. She was asking if I had contact info for any of his family. I don't but told her I'd ask around. Do you have anything?"

I had nothing, except lots of unknowns.

In the early days of COVID-19, Cadence, like many businesses, was forced to close for a couple months. Quite some time after we reopened, I realized we hadn't seen George, the Chattanooga shoe shiner, in quite a long time. I began to dig around online and found this very short obituary:

"George Truitt was born on November 10, 1946, and passed away on June 3, 2020 and is under the care of Chattanooga Funeral Home, Crematory & Florist-Valley View Chapel."

My heart was instantly weighted with so many unknowns. What happened to him? How did he die? Did he die alone? The only thing I learned was that no one claimed George's body, so he was unceremoniously laid to rest in a local cemetery for homeless or indigent folks in Chattanooga.

There are others.

She came in every day to get a cup of coffee from the Pay It Forward wall. He came in with her. She would ask for his coffee first, then hers. If there was only one Pay It Forward, she let him take it. On cold days, she would come in wrapped up in thin layers of blankets, coats, and hoodies. Her red knit gloves were more holes than gloves, certainly not enough to keep her hands warm. She could hardly hold her cup of coffee because her hands were shaking from the cold. She stood in front of the bar, her skin black from the soot from their campfire. Her hair was matted and wiry. She might take a shower once a week at the Community Kitchen, but it was obvious that showers were few and far between. He had ahold on her. She couldn't seem to break free.

He would treat her like dirt, and she would let him. The pair of them were the absolute picture of complete brokenness, rock bottom. I told her often that if she ever wanted out, we would help her. But she chose to stay. It was the only life she knew. She seemed to think that this was the life that she deserved, all that she would ever have. It's been months since I've seen her. No one knows where she is when I ask about her.

I could tell you more, so many more. Stories without endings. No happily ever afters. Unfinished chapters.

So much that is still … unknown.

18

Jesus Stuff

"All of this Jesus stuff."

Matthew's words still ring in my ears. Our conversation was unplanned and honest. He was trying to make sense of so many things. Trying to understand why his life had turned out the way it had. He reflected on good days and unpacked some of his darkest days. He tried to find ways to understand why a group of people like the folks at Cadence and RiverChurch would care so much for a random stranger who literally walked through the door after just being released from jail. He asked so many questions.

"Why?"

"How?"

He was wrestling the most with "the Jesus stuff."

"Shannon, what if you come to the end of your life, and you're wrong about it all? What if none of what you believed for all of these years is true?"

"Matthew, what if you come to the end of yours, and you're wrong?"

My faith teaches me that a life lived in unbelief, absent a relationship with God here and now, leads to an eternity absent a relationship with God as well—forever separated from God, with no hope of knowing Him or loving Him. That would be an eternity of hell, literally.

Eternity. That's a concept most of us cannot comprehend. Still, between the two of us—me believing in "all this Jesus stuff" and him not—it would be better for me if it were untrue that it would be for him if it were. This was a what-if I had come to terms with a long time ago and was at peace with.

Faith is a gift given to us to help us face the what-ifs in life. Faith is trusting in what cannot be seen or known for sure. Without faith, I'm left to face the unknowns of life, the what-ifs emptyhanded, without any hope, and a life lived without hope is dark, lonely, and miserable.

This was where Matthew found himself, in that dark, lonely, miserable place in life. I could look around me, sitting right there at that table in the corner in Cadence, and see so many miracles, so many times when things had happened in my life to fill my heart with hope. Those things all strengthened my faith, giving me the ability to face unknowns and what-ifs with grace and without fear.

Standing behind the bar of Cadence, I have encountered so many what-ifs, so many unknowns.

What if this whole coffee shop business thing flops?

What if people discover what I've been saying all along, that I don't have a clue how to run a business?

What if ... what if people take advantage of the help we offer them?

What if we give a homeless person a tent, and they turn right around and sell it for drugs?

What if we pour our lives into someone else's, and they walk away, disappear?

You have what-ifs too. We all do.

What if someone I love dies?

What if I lose my job?

What if the person I love and live with walks out on me?

What if my kids go down the wrong path?

We could fill volumes of books with what-ifs.

Unknowns and what-ifs can lead us to assumptions to fear the worst. They can cause us to withhold ourselves from others, choosing to not get involved in someone else's life, in an effort protect our own heart and personal interests.

Through my walk of faith, and especially in my role as a pastorista, I've learned that I'm not responsible for how the story—any story—ends, not even my own. I may see a happy ending, and I may not, but the end of the story isn't my responsibility. God writes the story, invites us to take a role in the story, and He determines the end. It's through faith that I live out my purpose—faith that He knows what He's doing and what will happen with Tim, with George, with Michael, with Matthew, and with me.

Years ago, a homeless man named Billy made his way into Cadence. He walked into RiverChurch one Sunday morning and sat down next to Mick, a RiverChurch family member who lovingly befriended him. Over the next few weeks, Billy became part of our family. He wasn't hard to love at all. Summer gave way to autumn, and nighttime temperatures began to grow cooler. One Sunday morning, another RiverChurch family member stopped me before worship and said they wanted to put Billy up in a hotel for a week. That morning, at the end of my sermon, I invited others to help provide a place for Billy to stay, and immediately others responded to my challenge.

Billy was sitting right in front of me when I made the announcement. He didn't see it coming. He had his fair share of unknowns and what-ifs. What if he lived the rest of his life on the streets? What would his future look like? So much unknown.

"Billy, you're not sleeping on a park bench tonight." He fell into a puddle of tears.

The next day, we invited Billy to come to Cadence to start a job that we created especially for him—stamping sleeves, breaking down boxes, wiping down tables. He came in late that Monday afternoon and told Jacob, "I woke up early today, but it's been so long since I've slept in a bed, so I just laid there until noon today!"

We started the process of helping him apply for government housing. Church folks brought him food and clothes. One afternoon, during his second week of staying in a hotel that his church family had provided for him, he came into work distraught.

A local police officer had tracked him down and told him that his sister on the other side of the state had been looking for him. He needed to call her immediately. He asked to use our phone, presuming why she had called. He knew his elderly father's health was failing, and he expected to hear the news that his dad had passed away.

When he finally reached his sister, his fears were confirmed; his dad had passed but almost three months earlier. The reason his sister was trying to reach him was because his father had left an inheritance for Billy, and she was telling him to come home to claim what was rightfully his.

At the end of the three weeks of his stay in a hotel, the exact amount of time we had paid for with the offerings and gifts of family members, Billy boarded a bus and moved home with his family to claim his inheritance. We haven't heard from Billy since.

What happened to him? Where is he now? Lots of unknowns, lots of what-ifs. Ours was never to determine the end of his story but to simply trust, to have faith that God had written Billy's story and that He had written in a role for us to play.

A week after my last conversation with Matthew, he called me, and I let his call go to voice mail. I was in a conversation with someone else and rationalized that I would talk to him later. He texted me the next day, but I didn't reply. We had a plan that I would pick him up the next Tuesday and drive him to an appointment. I expected we would talk then.

Sunday morning, Dean and Donna were at our gathering. They walked up to me afterward, asking for prayer. Donna had tears in her eyes.

"Shannon, my heart breaks for Matthew. I simply don't know what else to do for him. Please pray for us."

I did. I distinctly remember praying for God to give this mother and father peace—peace in their home, peace in their hearts, and peace for Matthew.

Later that afternoon, my phone woke me up from my usual Sunday-afternoon nap. It was Dean.

"Shannon! Shannon, Matthew is dead!"

A million questions flooded my mind.

What if I had taken his phone call last Thursday?
What if I had texted him back on Friday?
What if he didn't see Jesus when he died? What if he did?

I had no answers, and yet again I was left with so much of the unknown.

Matthew's parents asked me to speak at his memorial service at Cadence, and I struggled to know what to say. His story was blemished with so many dark moments. I would have to stand in front of family and friends and offer words of comfort. I begged God for wisdom as I prepared to look into the tearstained eyes of a brokenhearted mother and father with so many unknowns and what-ifs.

"There's a lot about Matthew's story I don't know. I don't know why things happened the way they did. I don't know why he was the way he was. But I know Jesus. I know Jesus brought Matthew here, to us, six months ago. I know He brought him here because He loved Matthew and He wanted him to see that this 'Jesus stuff' was real. I know that Jesus wanted to save Matthew's life. I don't know where Matthew is right now in the scope of eternity, but I know Jesus."

Matthew, Billy, George, Tim, Michael, and scores of other people whom I have met behind the bar—all of them remind me to bring my unknowns to Jesus. He takes my questions, my worries, my doubts, my fears, my stuff and exchanges it for His peace. I'm so thankful I know Jesus.

19

Help Wanted

Cadence had been operational for almost three years when we were forced to make decisions that would determine our very existence. In mid-2014, our lease ended abruptly at our original location. We had only a matter of weeks to build out and move to a new location just a few blocks away.

The day our property managers met with Brian and me to tell us that the owner had decided to terminate our lease, we walked out of that meeting in disbelief and disappointment. The property manager offered us a lead for another property owner who wanted a coffee shop to go into their space in the historic McConnell building a few blocks over from where we had been. We walked out from that meeting and immediately called that other property owner. We met him at the space on Seventh Street later that afternoon. Within a couple of days, we signed a new lease and began to make plans to move. We had a month to get out of the old space, so we closed that location two weeks after our termination meeting and set ourselves a goal of two weeks to get into the new location. We made the transition in the time frame we had set, but starting up in a new space just two blocks away was as challenging as starting from scratch.

Sales dropped drastically as we worked hard to rebuild our customer base. Two weeks felt like a lifetime, and our regular customers still needed their daily caffeine, and two weeks was just enough time for many of them to fall into a new routine or rhythm while Cadence was out of commission. It took us a long time to rebuild after reopening.

Brian generously kept infusing the business with cash each month to help make up the shortfall from drastically decreased sales. I had no extra capital to invest, so I kept pouring in sweat equity, doing everything I could to keep the doors open and customers coming. As 2014 came to an end, Brian and I were having more and more conversations about how we were going to survive. He couldn't keep pouring more money into a struggling business. We would have to make some hard decisions. We met with potential buyers, but no one seemed interested.

RiverChurch was using the space on weekends. Everything that I had poured my life into over the previous five years was packed tightly into four thousand square feet, and the what-ifs regarding our future were staring us in the face.

In mid-January, Brian decided to step away from Cadence. I'll never forget the night he called to tell me. He was gracious and honest, and I knew he truly wanted the best for everyone involved.

"I think we should close. But I know that's going to create some huge challenges for you and RiverChurch. So, we can keep trying to sell it, or simply just pull the plug altogether, or … if you want to take it, you can have it."

"Wait, what? Have Cadence?"

"Yeah, you don't have to buy me out. I would just release my portion of the business to you."

I couldn't breathe. I felt nauseous. I knew how to make coffee, how to pull shots of espresso, to steam milk, to offer great customer service, but I knew nothing about running a business. There was just no way. After all, I had come to Chattanooga to plant a church, not run a business. I pretty much turned down that offer in that conversation. We had already planned to have a meeting with the new property owners the next day to tell them we couldn't afford to stay open.

I went to bed with a heart weighted with dread and discouragement. It was all I could do to fight back the tears as I got into bed, telling Kristia about my conversation with Brian.

She listened intently. She could see the sadness in my eyes and hear it in my voice. Now Kristia isn't a coffee drinker. Hot chocolate is her jam, but she can't handle coffee. I've tried every sort of concoction to sweeten, flavor, cool, or spice it up, but every drink I have ever offered her brings the same puckered-up, slightly disgusted look to her face.

The past four years had been tough. Planting a church was hard enough, but starting a small business and having to be doubly on call twenty-four seven had certainly created some stressful times and led to disagreements, and even some feelings of abandonment on the home front. Part of her was almost relieved that some of the stress from the past four years might finally be going away.

We turned off the lights, and I lay there in the dark dealing with a flood of emotions. Failure.

Brokenhearted.

Grief.

Suddenly she turned on her lamp and sat up in the bed.

"I think we should take it. Keep it open. You and I, we will run it. Keep it open."

I sat up beside her. "Wait, what? Are you serious?"

We didn't have the money to keep infusing into the business. This decision would mean cutting our expenses drastically so we could stay open. The biggest expense was payroll, which meant we would have to let our entire staff go and immediately. How could we do that? Thankfully, the demographic of our staff was such that everyone could survive without their job at Cadence and could quickly and easily find employment elsewhere.

We had our meeting the next day, informing the property owners that Brian would be stepping away from Cadence and that Kristia and I would now step into full ownership. We met with our staff and explained the financial situation of the business, the immediate and necessary changes that would be made. Our entire staff was gracious and so understanding. All of them wanted to see Cadence survive with or without them working there.

The following Monday was Martin Luther King Day, so we took advantage of the federal holiday, and Kristia and I, along with all our kids and Kristia's sister Jacki, a former Starbucks barista, went into the shop to do a refresher on making drinks, running the register, and operating the café. The next day, we opened but under new management, so to speak.

From January to mid-March of that year, we opened, we closed, and we worked and worked and worked until our financials crossed from the red into the black. Makenzie, our oldest, was fourteen and homeschooled. In between reading, writing, and arithmetic, she learned the basics of coffee, how to pull shots, steam milk and make mean lattes. It wasn't child labor, I promise. We called it "workforce education."

Looking back over that entire year of 2015, I still wonder how we survived. But we did, and it was only because of the help of the Lord. I know that sounds cliché and what you would expect to hear from a pastor or preacher. But it's true. He helped us. He guided us. I had a long road of learning ahead of me, one that I'm still on today. My thinking had to change. My wording had to change. More than once, I made the statement, "I'm a pastor, not a small business owner." When I wasn't saying that, I could often be heard saying, "God didn't bring me here to run a business. He brought me here to plant a church."

I made that statement in the presence of a friend who is much more like a big sister to me. Gina and Kevin and their three kids stepped up beside us when we planted RiverChurch in 2009. Kevin and I had several phone calls and conversations about our calling to Chattanooga. A lifelong resident of the Scenic City, Kevin knew so much about the past, present, and future of Chattanooga. Before we ever moved to Chattanooga, we drove up from south Alabama for a daylong tour of the city, where Kevin took us to places, overlooks, key points from Missionary Ridge to downtown, out in the suburbs to help us have a better understanding of where God was leading us. The two of them, Kevin and Gina, were often the voices of reason and reminder, helping us keep focused on our purpose. They championed and cheered alongside of us with every step we took as RiverChurch was birthed, the same when Cadence opened, and when we stepped in as full owners of the café, they stepped right up with us. In one whine fest with Kevin and Gina, I made that same tired statement about God not bringing me here to run a business but to plant a church.

"Stop saying that."

Gina slapped me on the arm with a look of fury in her eyes.

"You're boxing Him in. He's obviously up to something here, and this business has literally been given to you. Who has a business given to them? He's brought you this far. You need help, and He's going to help you the rest of the way, and we will too!"

Her words were convicting and profound. Help wasn't just needed; it was wanted. Like an air traffic controller, Gina stepped up, recruited help, and directed them to the places where we needed the most help. She started coming on Tuesdays and working the cash register. Kevin would come on his lunch break and wash any dirty dishes. Others followed suit as my big sister recruited them to serve.

Mick joined the cause, as did Holly, Amy, Christine, Jessica, Ray and Sarah, and others. Each of these volunteers was a daily reminder that God had this under control. My unknowns about the future of Cadence, the what-ifs of how we would survive, were quietly laid to rest every time help walked through the door.

In our personal moments of what felt like crisis, uncertainty, and lots of fearfulness, I discovered the servant heart of Jesus in a new and refreshing way, as demonstrated by our closest and dearest friends. In them, I saw Him, lightening our load and restoring our hope for the future of Cadence. Once again, there was Jesus, standing with me behind the bar, extending a hand of help through fellow followers.

Even after Cadence was able to afford payroll again, these willing workers came faithfully, constantly, and ready to serve. This was the kind of help I wanted, the help I needed.

20

Get It

"Hi, I'm Lynn, and I would love to volunteer here at Cadence."

I didn't know this lady at all. She seemed nice enough. She had a pleasant countenance and an assertiveness that was refreshing. At the time, I was desperate for more help. We were working hard to keep our payroll expenses down and were trying to utilize some volunteer help daily. We never expected that any of our volunteers would be committing for life, so we weren't surprised, saddened a little but not surprised, when a volunteer had to say goodbye.

"Come on. We'll take any help we can get."

I don't normally bring people behind the bar on an impulse, but something about this lady seemed like a risk that was worth taking.

She offered us her help three days a week. Day one, she stepped up to the sink and washed dishes, swept the floors, and cleaned the bathrooms, and that was all in her first hour. OK, that's a slight exaggeration, but she swept in with an efficiency and diligence that would soon make her irreplaceable. I've often said that someone would have to pry her from my cold, dead hands before I would let her leave our Cadence family.

Lynn caught on fast. She became a pinch hitter when we were short-staffed and hit with a rush of customers. She stepped in like a substitute teacher when a staff member would call in sick. Still today, Lynn does just about everything at Cadence. She bakes, she waits on customers, she helps us with inventory, she answers phones, she keeps the staff on their toes, ensuring we do our dead level best to maintain a high standard of excellence and customer service. I could go on and on and on, telling you what she does around here. Often, customers will assume she's the owner; she's that much of a fixture at Cadence. I particularly like that, especially when a salesperson comes calling, I've given her full authority and permission to impersonate me as much as she wants to simply shake them off.

I wish you could see my text message inbox. Seventy-five percent are from her—reminding me, filling me in, letting me know of something she "took care of, so you don't have to." I literally could go away for a week, and Lynn would make sure that everything kept running smoothly. I have, and she has.

For all that she does behind the bar, I'm particularly thankful for the times that Lynn has come out from behind the bar to help a person who has walked into the shop with some sort of a need. She gets it. When you walk into Cadence, the first thing you see on the front left wall are our three core values: coffee, community, and change. We see the opportunity to serve coffee as an opportunity to build community and to bring lasting change in people's lives. I think it's that kind of culture that brought Lynn to us in the first place. From day one, she embraced who we are as a coffee shop, and from that day to this, she does all that she does so that we can be about what we say that we are about. At times, she's even enlisted the help of her husband, Brian, who is just as much a servant as she is. On more than one occasion, I've seen or heard of the two of them going to a customer's apartment or house to take them food, help them build a set of stairs, or bring them furniture.

About the same time that Lynn came to Cadence as a volunteer, so did Ray and Sarah. I had known of this couple for quite a while. We attended the same church many years earlier. Their daughter and Kristi grew up in the same youth group. I'm not sure what inspired them to come volunteer at Cadence, but, like Lynn, they became pillars for me in some of my most challenging days. Ray is a retired engineer who welcomes the impossible.

When we needed an appliance repaired,
Ray knew exactly how to fix it.

When we needed storage shelves,
Ray delivered every time.

When we decided to add an outdoor bar,
Ray was on it.

When we were hungry for a delicious Reuben,
Ray brought the corned beef and shared his delectable "Ray's Reuben."

Sarah, his wife, always says, "Where there's a will, there's a Ray." She's right. Both Ray and Sarah, they get it too. They understood that we wanted to be so much more than just a coffee shop, and every Wednesday, they would show up to help us be just that.

I always looked forward to Wednesdays when Ray and Sarah would come, truthfully because of the helping hands they brought but also because of the presence they brought with them. I can still hear their spirited voices when a customer would walk in.

Their hello and "How are you today?" were always filled with such joy. They always made the room feel happy and light. They were also sensitive to people who would come in needing more than just a cup of coffee.

On a weekday outside of her normal Wednesday, Sarah came to Cadence for a meeting and noticed a young man sitting on the couch, wearing a backpack and holding a bus ticket. He seemed more like a little boy in his demeanor than the actual young adult that he was. Sarah met eyes with the guy, and they politely acknowledged each other. Her appointment was a bit late, so she decided to sit at one of the tables near the couches. She couldn't help but notice how the young man seemed to look nervously around the room, as if he were looking for someone. A few minutes passed, and he got up and wandered to Sarah sitting at the table. She initially thought he was coming to her to ask for money, but instead he asked if she could tie his shoe. The man's left arm was paralyzed, and he needed help with this basic task.

Sarah smiled her typical fairylike smile and asked with that typical sparkle in her voice, "A single or a double knot?" He chose a double.

"I think I need a wife," he said with a laugh.

"That or just a good friend," she replied with a smile and a twinkle in her eyes.

"I'm just thankful I got to be that friend to him," Sarah later told me as she shared her story.

Serving people behind the bar or on the other side of the bar came naturally for Ray and Sarah. Whether pouring a cup of coffee, hanging a shelf, tying a shoe, or offering a single young lady a tissue and a shoulder to cry on, Ray and Sarah got it. They knew the heartbeat of Cadence, and that heartbeat kept the same rhythm as their own.

Behind the Bar

I was sitting at a table with some guys from RiverChurch one day when a guy in his early twenties walked up to our table, stretched out his hand, and introduced himself.

"Hi, Shannon. You don't know me. My name is Cody, and I would like to work at Cadence."

"Nice to meet you, Cody. Let's get you an application."

He looked the part. He had a hipster sort of vibe. A thin, seemingly slightly undernourished sort of kid, complete with Vans, a beanie, and a sparse yet scruffy beard. I hired Cody shortly after his impromptu introduction and watched with amazement as this guy seemed to find his sweet spot. A quick learner, Cody caught on fast and soon became one of the best baristas to ever stand behind the bar at Cadence. Like many guys his age, he had walked through his stages of rebellion, seeking out his purpose in life. He told me how he came to faith in Jesus one day while standing in the shower. He decided then and there to follow Him and has followed Him ever since. Cody didn't just capture both the art and science of coffee; he caught the culture of Cadence. He welcomed customers, dealt with unruly stragglers, mentored new employees, and practically ran the shop exactly as I would, at times even better. Cody had a dream to open and operate his own coffee shop one day. He held tightly to that dream, and in short order, Cody's dream became a reality.

Just a few weeks ago, I was on the other side of town for an appointment. I hadn't had my morning cup of coffee yet, so I stopped by a relatively new coffee shop. It's beautiful inside—clean, sleek, inviting. I could see myself camping out there for hours on end if I could. The operator met me as I walked through the door. It was Cody. He left the table he was wiping down and walked right up to me and hugged me. He hasn't changed that much outwardly, still slightly undernourished with that sparse yet scruffy beard. He's got a few new tattoos on his arm, and he's traded his Vans for Chelsea boots. He's married now and a dad. I took a second to just look at him, to take it all in. He was in his element, and I felt like a proud dad. Proud because he gets it.

What did he get? It's the same thing that Lynn and Ray and Sarah and so many others get when they step behind the bar at Cadence. I like to think they saw Jesus using this café to impact the lives of others. They understood that it is possible to live with Jesus, to be like Jesus, to do what Jesus did not just within the four walls of a church building, or only on Sunday, but wherever you find yourself, even behind the bar of a coffee shop.

They get it.

21

Hard Day

Many people often romanticize the coffee shop environment. I did. I often said that if I could work every day in a coffee shop, I would get so much work done. I love the chill environment, the ambient noise of an espresso machine steaming milk, the aroma of fresh brewed coffee, music that's less elevator and more lo fi. It is a cool place to work. *Cool.* Now that's a word I've heard often.

"I've always had a dream to own my own coffee shop one day. I think it would be so cool."

If I had a nickel for every time I've heard that statement or something close, I could most certainly take my wife to a nice dinner at Ruth's Chris. I never want to be the guy who busts anyone's dream bubble, but sometimes I wish I could show them a collection of video clips of those less-than-ideal days that I've had the privilege to live through and learn from.

Payroll.
Bills.
Inventory, getting too much of one thing or not enough of another.
Taxes. You wouldn't believe the number of different taxes and the amount you have to pay every year.

Irritable customers.

I could build a list that would fill an entirely separate book. Suffice it to say, we've seen some very hard days.

Take for instance the day most recently when I got quite the tongue-lashing from a guy who was sitting out front smoking. We have a No Smoking sign posted at our outdoor bar. When we see someone smoking, we politely ask them to step across the street to a picturesque little alley called Cooper's Alley. It's a pleasant place where a smoker can be far enough away from our entrance and enjoy some local art. This fellow was sitting at the bar, and as always, I kindly asked that he not smoke there.

"You're gonna need to back off, man!" he said with a rapid rise in volume.

"I'm having a really bad day, and you're not making it any better." By now, he was at full rage capacity and had a growl in his voice.

"I'm grateful for the free cup of coffee, but I ain't taking your junk, man!"

He dropped a few F bombs and a few other incomprehensible phrases and got up and walked away. I went back into the shop to the meeting from which I had just excused myself, calmly gesturing to the onlookers inside that everything was OK.

There was also that day when Tony came into Cadence for his Pay It Forward coffee. He's a mystery to me. Somedays, he comes in and is kind and conversant and pleasant. Other days, most days in fact, he comes in like a ticking time bomb. Problem is he doesn't have any big red countdown numbers on his person to let you know when he's going to explode. I had a conversation with him one day about his practice of yelling and getting worked up for no apparent reason. He would get his coffee and sit down at a seat and for a few minutes seem to be calm and collected. Then, without warning, he would shout, screech, or flat-out scream. He apologized and said it was because of the voices in his head. He said he would control it better.

One morning, there was no shouting, screeching or screaming. He just abruptly stood up from his seat, walked up to our solid glass door, and shoved it wide open, making the most raucous commotion. He set out walking down the street, swinging his arms wildly. I followed him.

"Tony! Are you OK?"

He turned around and looked at me with a bit of a death stare, and then he started making some crazy noises.

"Hey, man, I can't have you slamming my door like that. You could break it!"

He didn't like that at all. He took the lid off his cup of coffee and started charging my direction. The next thing I knew, I was ducking and dodging a hot cup of coffee. I wonder if he was ever a pitcher. He's got a good arm.

He later came back and apologized, and I cautiously agreed to let him come back in for another cup of coffee. He kept himself under control for a couple of days until about a week later, when I saw him reach into the tip jar and swipe a couple of dollar bills.

"I saw you take that money. Put it back."

He denied it. "Don't know what you're talking about."

"Put it back or leave." That's all it took to trigger him.

He swung at me, grazing my nose. That was the last straw. He can't come back. He's tried, but I meet him at the door. He looks at me curiously, then turns around and walks off.

Donald came in one day and got crass with a couple of ladies on staff at Cadence. They texted me and told me about his nasty tirade, and a couple of days later, I met him on the sidewalk as he was about to come into the shop.

"Hey, man, I heard you got pretty mad at the girls on Saturday when you came in for coffee. Is that true?"

"Yeah! They made me mad."

"Well, I don't care how mad they made you; you're not going to be disrespectful to those ladies. Do you understand? We're here to serve you, but we don't have to if you're going to talk to them like that."

Donald didn't like that. I got a personal concert of the same belligerent song and dance he had performed a couple of days earlier. He was making up swear words I had never heard before. He even said things about my mom that I couldn't understand, but I knew he wasn't talking nicely about her. He hasn't been back.

Wiley was a Cadence regular for quite a while. He's a mixture of creeper and Captain Hook. He has a wife he's never met who lives in Asia, a daughter who's a "big star" in Russia, and apparently, he has some connection to Hillary Clinton. He showed up at church one Sunday and started watching some pretty sketchy videos, and a guy standing behind him asked him to turn it off. He got mad and pulled out a shank right there in the middle of "Amazing Grace." I saw he was making quite the commotion, so I got his attention and firmly motioned for him to leave. He left but not before spitting on Kevin, who had picked up a chair like a lion tamer to keep a distance from him. He walked back by Cadence the next day and started to walk in when I met him at the door.

"Wiley, you can't come back in here, and you know why."

"I don't want to come in. I just came to tell you that I'm reporting this place. I've already called Hillary Clinton, and she's going to shut this place down." Hillary never called, and we're still open.

I could tell you about the flamethrower who stood across the street in Cooper's Alley, literally running up a wall, screaming at us from across the street that he was going to "burn this place to the ground." Or about Wendell, who was sitting around the corner from Cadence the other day and stopped me when I walked by, asking me what the Bible said about caring for the poor. I told him that it said we should.

"Then why don't you?" he asked.

I couldn't believe his question. This was the same guy for whom we bought clothes so he could work at a restaurant downtown. He never showed up for the job. Later, he asked for help with a bus ticket to get to another part of the state; he had work lined up there, so we got him a ticket and sent him on his way, only for him to show up a month or two later, saying the job didn't work out. He then came back in the shop asking for a pair of clothes and shoes because all his stuff had been stolen. We gave him clothes and shoes, and there he sat asking me why we didn't help the poor. I simply walked away from that pointless discussion.

Then there was the guy who stripped down completely naked and decided to bathe in the girl's bathroom. Our barista Joy called me that Saturday afternoon in tears.

"I don't get paid enough to have to deal with this."

We put locks with keys on the bathroom doors before Monday morning and made our restrooms for paying customers only.

We've had more than one disgruntled customer who decided to pee in the corner, and a lady who walked right into one of the glass panes in front of the store. She thought it was a door. According to her, our windows were too clean, and we would be hearing from her lawyer.

Granted, most of these instances are likely unique to us, and many other coffee shops might not have to deal with the same kinds of folks, but it's real, live scenarios like these that can certainly diminish the cool factor of working or owning your own café.

Thankfully, the good days outnumber the hard days, but make no mistake the coffee shop world isn't always as cool or as dreamy as some might think. Even in those days, those really hard days, I've had to learn to stop, breathe, and remember Jesus experienced hard days just like these. Sometimes the hard days make me wonder if it's worth it. I've literally laid in the bed some mornings and pleaded with God like a fourth grader not wanting to go to school that day. "Do I have to go back behind the bar today?" Despite my whiny voice and my attempts to hide under the covers, I'm reminded that Jesus always showed up, even on the hard days. He gives me grace to go back behind the bar. He, also gives me stories to look back on and at least chuckle, if I can't fully laugh about them.

22

Ordinary

Not every day at Cadence is filled with crisis, drama, or flying cups of coffee. Most days at 11 East Seventh Street are … ordinary. No two days are the same. Some days are busier. Others are slower, but in every day, there is still some cadence.

An ordinary day usually begins with a few of my buddies from the gym stopping by for their first cup of the day. Burt, Paul, and another tagalong or two stop in with them. We talk about how hard the five o'clock workout was and the day ahead of each of us. Our banter doesn't last long before they're out the door with a hearty "See ya in the mornin'!"

Seven in the morning seems to be prime time for small groups of men. It may be a Bible study, a book club, or just a few fellas catching up with their buddies. I have a cup of coffee with Tim every other Monday morning. I have another cup of coffee later in the week with Jacob. On Tuesdays, I meet with Ben, Brandon, Cameron, Damon, Harrison, Michael, Sam and Tim. We check in with one another and encourage one another. Somedays we even get mad at one another and make the rest of the group feel awkwardly out of place. We'll hug it out and look forward to the next Tuesday morning.

Nick will typically stop in somewhere around eight. He's like a treasure box of surprises. You never know what he's going to tell you. Today he was showing me his new-to-him Mitsubishi Montera that he bought for a thousand bucks. He updates me on Christopher and how tall he is now and how he's doing in school. He'll inevitably start into a story that gets interrupted at least two or three times by someone else needing to ask me a question or his phone ringing at the highest, most annoying volume possible. The entire room knows who's calling him too, because he has his phone set to announce, again at the highest, most annoying volume possible, with a robotic blare, "Phone call from Gary."

"This is Nick," he announces. The entire room seems to be invited into his conversation, whether they want to be or not.

He picks his story back up with his classic "Long story longer …" and continues telling me whatever he's super jazzed up about. He'll get a cup of coffee, maybe a double shot of espresso. He even asks for a dollop of whipped cream in that double shot if he's having a particularly good morning. He always seems to tell me goodbye for the entire day, but I don't worry; I know he'll be back in two or three times again that same day.

By now, the banks around us are about to open, so the bankers and bank tellers walk down Seventh to their respective branches. A handful stop in for a cup of coffee, an English muffin sandwich, a sausage cream cheese popover, or a bagel, and then they're off to their world of nickels and dimes.

Ms. Gail usually makes her trek down our street about the same time. She's the administrative assistant for an interestingly disheveled lawyer. She keeps him in line, or at least that's what she attempts to do. She gets a cup of coffee, maybe a sandwich, and from time to time, she asks about a new homeless friend who may be frequenting Cadence as of late.

"Who's the new guy?" she asks.

I'll tell her his story, and generally she'll buy his breakfast—anonymously. She learned the hard way. One fella thought she was trying to pick him up once when she bought him a breakfast sandwich.

"I had a hard time shaking him off, but he eventually got the message I wasn't looking for love," she says with a hearty laugh.

"Thanks, Ms. Gail, for caring for our homeless friends."

"Are you kidding? They're my people. That's who God wants me to love. Thanks for giving me a way to do it." Then off she goes to keep her boss organized for another day.

Ms. Tammy works next door at the United Way. Her drink of choice is a dirty chai. She just stopped for a quick conversation as she was heading back to work.

"I talked to your daughter Makenzie the other day. She was telling me how she had a heart for missions and hoped to carry on your legacy someday, maybe in another country somewhere. I looked her in the eyes and told her, 'Makenzie, you're carrying on your dad's legacy right here.' Her face lit up like Christmas, Shannon!"

I smiled as I fought back a tear or two.

Today is Tammy's son's birthday. He would have been thirty-eight today. He passed away unexpectedly a couple of years ago. I can still see how much she misses him, even in her smile.

"I'm praying for you today, Ms. Tammy. Praying your day is filled with joy as you think about your son."

"It already is, coming here, talking to you. It all reminds me that God is good, and I'm just passing through."

Carl will be in a little later. He works with Tammy next door. He's always so chipper and smiling. I think he may have been a pastor back in the day. I could be wrong, but he has that air about him. We talk about Chattanooga Lookout Baseball; he asks about my son and if he's still playing baseball. He calls me "Jamie." Not sure how that happened. Pre-COVID, he always called me "Shannon." I don't mind though. We pastor types tend to be bad with names.

Marty and Lloyd will be in later in the day. They're brothers. Both attorneys. They never seem to come in at the same time; one always seems to be a few minutes behind the other. There's no denying that they are brothers, between their nonstop bantering and the fact that they look so much alike. One says he's older. The other says he's better looking. Marty gets a twelve-ounce coffee but sometimes changes it up between medium and dark roast. He always gets his coffee black though.

"I'll take it black, black like a lawyer's soul." He grins.

His soul isn't black. He's a follower of Jesus, and once a week, you'll find him here with some of his lawyer buddies discussing their latest book and praying for one another. I can always count on them to replenish our Pay It Forward board with a few extra cups of coffee.

If it's a Tuesday or Thursday, we can always expect the "Y Ladies." That's the name we've given to them because they come downtown for their midmorning class at the Y. Then they walk over to Cadence for a cup of coffee, where they sit and cackle and talk about what crazy things their husbands are doing and what their kids are up to. Their drink choices range from hot tea to a chocolate chai, or black coffee and sometime black coffee poured over ice. They don't let us get away with much either. One day, Clara ordered "coffee poured over ice," and Mady, my daughter, rang her up for a regular cup of coffee and gave her a glass of ice. Bea was next in line, and she ordered an "iced coffee," so Mady rang her up for cold brew, which is what we call iced coffee. There was considerable price difference between what Clara had ordered and what Bea had ordered, and Bea was a little perturbed.

"Why did you charge me more? We ordered the same thing?"

Mady was a little stunned. She was just ringing in what they had separately asked for. She didn't really know how to respond. This was her first customer-service job, so she tried to maintain the highest level of customer service and then came to me to tell me what happened.

I walked over to Bea and Clara and the other Y ladies and explained that cold brew is made through a more intensive and expensive process. They were fine.

"Thanks for explaining, Shawn." Bea calls me "Shawn." Again, I don't mind. When we were foster parenting and walking through adoption, these ladies were like a group of watchful grandmothers. They asked for updates each week and left gift cards for baby clothes. They loved us and loved well.

Travis is a bank vice president, so he comes in later in the morning for his sugar-free caramel macchiato and a new idea we should try to get more customers.

Mary Lynn pulls up outside and politely comes for her cold brew with sugar-free hazelnut and heavy whipping cream.

"Have a blessed day" is her typical parting blessing.

Off and on throughout the day, we'll have various folks come in and camp out at a table for an hour or two, even more. We'll get to know them and hear their stories. Then they'll move along to other coffee shops around town for a change of scenery.

Harry is a contractor for the Tennessee Valley Authority, and Cadence is his office. He's a coffee club member, so he pays for his coffee up front for the year. He bounces around from place to place in the café, often rearranging furniture to his liking. It bugged me at first. Now I laugh and look forward to seeing where Harry will land today and what new arrangement he will create with a café table or comfortable reading chair.

Sam usually stops by mid to late afternoon, and as usual, he's "normal."

Of course, salt and peppered into our day, we generally have an interesting character or two come in for a Pay It Forward. There's Patrick, who's counting down the days until he meets up with his soul mate, Shania Twain. There's Anthony, who stands out in front of our door holding his pants up with one hand while he busts a move or two before he walks in for his cup of coffee.

"Anthony, you can't stand there and dance in front of my door. You'll scare customers away."

He smiles.

"Sorry. Got any Pay It Forwards?" We generally do. He's still smiling as he leaves.

Charlie is a regular too. Now he's an interesting one. Something about him reminds me of Ray Charles. I suppose it's his dark glasses. For the longest time, I thought he was blind, but I don't think that's the case. He's quiet. He likes his coffee sweet—super, super sweet—and with lots of cream. He then sits at a table for hours. He'll come back up for his refill; we give one refill for Pay It Forwards. Then, after he's had his Pay It Forward and his refill, he buys a cup of coffee. He'll drink that and then come back up for his free refill on that cup of coffee. I know some would say he's taking advantage of a good thing, and they're probably right. But we're his place, a safe place, so we don't make a big deal about it.

One day, Charlie had eaten something at the Community Kitchen that "tore his insides up," as he would later report. He hurriedly made his way to our restroom and came out quite some time later. Things had not gone all that well for him in the restroom, so he came out and told our cashier

"Um ... I may have made a bit of a mess in there."

"We'll handle it," she told him.

I walked back to the restroom and could tell before opening the door that he had made more than a bit of a mess. It was a big mess. I'll spare you the details, but it was a bad situation—a three masks and three pairs of gloves kind of situation. He came back in the next day, and I sat down with him to make sure he was OK.

"You left me a big old mess yesterday," I told him.

"I know. I know I did. And can I tell you? That was never supposed to happen!"

I agreed with him.

It's fine though. That kind of thing doesn't happen often. But in a weird sort of way, it is kind of part and parcel of what ordinary looks like around here.

23

FAMILY AFFAIR

Cadence is a family-owned and -operated business. My wife and I are listed as the official owners, but each of our five kids has some sort of vested interest in this beautifully complicated and challenging venture. Kristi oversees our scheduling, interior design and presentation, and supervises my ability or lack thereof to balance work and home life. Makenzie is presently our Seventh Street manager. She's a former Chick-fil-A employee, so she brings a wealth of quality customer-service experience to the table. Madilynn is a cashier and up-and-coming barista who's just learning to like coffee—the sweeter and more loaded with chocolate, the better. Josie is part of our baking team. I know I'm her dad, but I think she has a gift. She's good at what she does. She loves exploring ideas for new food offerings. She's a bit sneaky though. If I time my visit to the kitchen just right, I'll happen upon her while she's doing a bit of taste testing, or quality control as she calls it. Jayden is my mini-me, but he's more of a charmer with the older ladies.

"Your dress looks lovely today." That always melts a few hearts.

"I like your hat" is generally his greeting to the rare Yankees fan who stops by.

Ari brings the cuteness factor to the table. She bounces in with mom on inventory days, carrying a few grocery items. It's hard work, and it doesn't come free. We generally must pay her with a kid-size and kid-temp hot chocolate.

Cadence has brought its fair share of stress to the family from time to time, but for the most part, it really has become home away from home. It has also been the source of lots of extended family members. I know it sounds a bit cliché, but I really do see our team of employees as more than just employees. They very much so are like family to us. Most of all our current employees are young enough to be our kids, and Kristia and I love them like our kids. They annoy us sometimes, like our kids. Trying to schedule them to work shifts with all their time-off requests and "I'm not feeling well, I may have Covid" texts can become a bit daunting, but we know full well that we couldn't do anything from Cadence if it wasn't for this team of quality men and women.

I often reflect on our interviews with our very first employees and laugh. We really had no idea what we were doing when we interviewed them. We acted like we did, but once we hired them, I don't think we fooled them for long. But from that day to this, for the most part, Cadence has always been blessed with salt of the earth kind of people to stand behind our bar. We've had a few dark days. There was that one time when a manager from another coffee shop in town crept in and offered an employee a job. They took the offer and about three or four other employees with them. I had to get over my hurt feelings in that situation and adopt the mentality that it is just business.

As an employer, we've always sought to hire team members who could help us be the best in customer service that we could possibly be. What Chick-fil-A lacks in healthy food, they more than make up for in customer service. I've often said that my dream is for

Cadence to be the Chick-fil-A of coffee. Their success has rested on the shoulders of quality employees who know how to offer second-mile service—going above and beyond what is expected to make a customer's experience five-star worthy on any review page. We've had our fair share of misses and one-star moments, but for the most part, our team nails it every time.

We have also wanted to create a place where people can come and grow, excel, and become a better version of themselves than they were when they started working for us. I remember our interview with one of our first employees, Natasha. She was young, not too far out of high school. She was dating one of the guys who played in the band of our worship team at RiverChurch. She arrived for her interview fifteen minutes earlier and sat nervously in her car until the exact moment that her interview was to start. She walked in, sat down, noticeably nervous, and later breathed a sigh of relief when we hired her. She came with no coffee experience and left as one of the best baristas in the city. She left Cadence and went on to work in other cafés and expand her horizons to baking and creating amazing dishes that could go on any high-end restaurant menu in the city. The thing I was most grateful for was the front-row seat I had to Tasha's growth and development. I watched this nervous high school grad become a mature and trustworthy team player on our staff. I performed her wedding ceremony and watched her become a wife, and a mom to two beautiful kids. Tasha has been gone for a long time from Cadence, but if we had a wall of family photos of our employees, hers would certainly be there.

Jacob came to work for Cadence after serving with a mission's organization in Australia for two years. He grew and developed as a man, a barista, a leader, a general manager, a husband, and now a dad right in front of our eyes. His grade school sweetheart became his wife, and before long, she became part of our family too. The two of them worked together on staff at Cadence until Jacob went to work for our coffee roaster, but Rachel stayed on and stepped up as my assistant who keeps me from making a massive mess of things and reminds me where I've left my keys. We've even become pseudo-coffee-grandparents since their little boy was born. I like to say that their little guy is a "Little BIT" (Barista in Training).

I know, to some, working in a coffee shop might look like a walk in the park kind of job, and maybe in some cases it is. But to be a family member at Cadence, you must be cut from a different kind of cloth. Sure, you have to deal with your occasional irritable customer who ordered a cappuccino and it wasn't foamy enough. There's always that one customer who comes in at the last minute and orders five pour overs for their closest friends. They also have to deal with the customer who wants a half-caf, nonfat, no foam, sugar-free vanilla latte, heated to 110, oh yeah with an extra shot of "expresso," which by the way at their coffee shop back home was a personalized drink that some poor barista named after them, which makes perfect sense as to why they would come in and ask for it by name here at Cadence.

"Yeah, I'll take a large Connie." (I'm rolling my eyes right now.)

Those challenges are not unique to the role of barista or cashier at Cadence. But what our family of employees do have to deal with here that they would less likely deal with in other places are the unpredictable moments when a homeless person who's had too much to drink walks in and unloads a barrage of profanities on them. They have the tough job of telling a potentially volatile person sitting on our sofas that they can't sleep there or leave their every worldly possession sitting in the middle of the floor. They've been flashed, flipped off, spit on, ogled, harassed, and yelled at, and yet they keep coming back to serve.

Not every employee of Cadence is or has been a follower of Jesus. That's never been a requirement. When I interview potential employees, I share enough of the Cadence story with them so they understand that we are a faith-friendly environment. But I never make their declaration of faith in Jesus a hiring requirement. Here's the thing. Some of our employees have needed to see a better example of Jesus too. Countless Cadence employees have been hurt, emotionally and spiritually burned, beaten and bruised by folks who call themselves Christians. Jesus has needed to be just as obvious behind the bar among our employees as He has to the customers who walk through our door.

Looking back over our years of operation, I can count on one hand the times when we've had an employee who didn't get it. They couldn't seem to find either the rhythm or the culture of Cadence. But even in those instances, they weren't bad people; they just didn't fit. Their time with us was probably short-lived, but my hope even for them is that their time at Cadence helped them to grow and be that better version of themselves.

I kind of wish I did have a wall of family photos of all our Cadence employees, both past and present. I can't think of one person who has worked with us that I wouldn't want their picture on that wall, because the way I see it, Cadence isn't just a coffee shop. It's a family affair.

24

Lean

"Shannon, I've never seen God cover anyone's tail like He covers yours."

Those are the words that Lynn has often said to me when we've made it through uncertain times or choppy waters. Truer words have never been spoken. I've told you that my degree was in sociology, that I moved to Chattanooga to plant a church, not to run a business. So many times, I have found myself in over my head with questions and uncertainties. Countless sleepless nights have left me praying to the point of tears, "God, please don't let me mess this up." I've made some dumb decisions as a business owner, and some of those decisions could have been dumb enough to take us out. But God.

Other circumstances, beyond my control, have also given rise to significant fear and anxiety over the livelihood of this business and how we would survive.

Not long after we moved to our new location on Seventh Street, the street itself was closed for two days. Day one brought some work crews to our street to cut down two massive trees, and the next day, our street was closed for the Armed Services Parade. The parade was around the corner on Market Street, but our street was used strictly for parking for dignitaries who would be sitting in the grandstands around the corner at the county courthouse. We needed the business badly, and the second day when I walked outside the store to a blocked-off street, I wanted to curl up in the fetal position and cry. I walked back inside whispered a quick, "Oh, Lord, please help us today" prayer, and in a few minutes, a customer came in—then another, then another—and before long, we had a line that backed up all the way to the front door. In fact, we were slammed with a line of drinks for well over an hour. We practically sold out of all our pastries. We even broke a record for highest morning sales!

I journaled about another time when things were uncertain, and I woke up at 2:27 in the morning and couldn't go back to sleep because the noise of questions clanging around in my head was deafening.

"What am I going to do about …?"

"How am I going to pay for …?"

"Did I remember to …?"

"When am I going to be able to …?"

Business was slow at the time. It was a hot summer. We had seen 104-degree temperatures for what seemed like days, and no one wanted to be out in the heat. No iced latte or cold brew was worth weathering that heat.

Our street was a construction zone. Progress was all around us, but it felt like it was killing us. Work trucks took up every parking spot in front of our shop. Our regular customers were frustrated at the lack of parking and would drive on to another coffee shop to get their caffeine fix.

It was a lean time. Lean times have a way of causing me to freak out.

"Oh no! What am I not doing?"

"Is God punishing me?"

I start begging forgiveness for everything—all my sins of commission as well as my sins of omission.

But I always seem to come back to a place of remembering the faithfulness of God to that point, how he helped us come this far. I would lie there in my bed in the dark room and simply pray, "Help me trust You more."

Not long after that, I was out for an early-morning run downtown, praying for a miracle.

"God, I'm just asking for one small miracle. Would You lighten this stress load? I'm not going to ask You for something specific. I just need your help. God, I need a small miracle!"

I ran past Seventh Street, and suddenly I came to a screeching stop. The barricades, the barrels, the work trucks, the reflector lights—all of it was gone. Our street was open again, and that meant customers would be coming back by again. He heard my prayer.

The scariest of all days though was the day when the mayor of Chattanooga issued an executive order for all nonessential businesses to be closed because of COVID-19. Now, I could argue that coffee was essential to the well-being of all Chattanoogans, but it would have been a wasted effort. Downtown was a ghost town. Everyone was already staying home, sheltering in place.

I drove down to Cadence to put a Closed until Further Notice sign on the door, and I was heartsick.

Behind the Bar

I sat there in the empty store and reflected over our story. I remembered how Cadence had started as a what-if idea more than ten years earlier and eventually became a reality that was, quite literally, handed to Kristia and me. I remembered how we ran the store, just Kristia, Makenzie, and I, for three months and how people stepped up beside us to help keep the doors open then.

God had been faithful to us. After all, the story of Cadence wasn't really our story; we were just characters in the story. No, this was a story that only God could have written, and yet I wondered if this was how it was going to end.

While the streets outside were as silent as the café inside, I sat in a chair at a table and thought about Abraham in the Bible. God gave him a son, Isaac. Isaac was an "unlikely" in Abraham and Sarah's life, just as unlikely as Cadence had been for Kristia and me. Then, years after Isaac was born, God challenged Abraham to lay Isaac on an altar, to offer him as a sacrifice. Abraham obeyed. Or at least he got as far as lifting a knife over his son's young body, until God stopped him and provided a ram in a nearby thicket as the actual sacrifice, and well … the rest is history.

I wondered if Abraham slept much the night before he put Isaac on the altar. I wondered if he shed a tear in the dark hours of the night, knowing what he would be expected to do the next day. I wondered if he had that sick feeling in his stomach, you know the one that precedes doing something that you know you have to do but dread doing. I wondered how he held it together. Did he ask God, "Why?"

I did.

I wasn't sure I could lay Isaac on the altar. Our Isaac was more than just a coffee shop. Cadence has always been more than just a coffee shop. So much more. It was the place where I had discovered my

141

true purpose in life, where I had the chance to write my own job description, come up with my own job title.

It was a gathering place, a modern-day well. A place where friendships had been birthed. Here I had invested in people's lives, and they had invested in mine.

It brought Nick and Christopher and Nick's best friend, Gary. I had met Billy, and Peterson, and Sam, and Gene, and George, and Clayton, and Paul, and Ronnie, and Moses, and Joshua, and Raymond, and "the other Gary (the drunk one)," and Gail (the sweet one who worked for the disheveled lawyer), and "the other Gayle" (who's just a little bit scary). I could list names of people from customers, staff, and volunteers.

Cadence had been the Monday-through-Saturday extension of the church God brought us to Chattanooga to plant. It was ground zero for RiverChurch to engage in marketplace ministry. It was the trenches where our church family stepped into and locked arms with Kristia and me to care for the people who would come stumbling through our doors.

It was the place where our kids had grown up, standing behind the bar, barely able to see over it. The place where they pretended to take care of customers and make their lattes. Cadence was the place where Kristia and I would go sit sometimes after hours and just talk, dream, laugh, and pray.

Cadence was so much more than a coffee shop, but that day, it was our Isaac. That day, I had to lay this beautiful, unlikely gift that God had given us on the altar and trust ... simply trust Him to write the rest of this story, even if this was the end of it.

Once again, I found myself in a place of huge unknowns. I asked the same questions other small business owners were asking.

"Will we open again?"
"Will we survive?"

At that moment, I didn't know.

But ...
I knew Jesus.

I knew I had to lean on Him. I knew that He had a plan. I knew that He knew what He was doing. I knew that He was good. I knew that if He asked me to lay Isaac on the altar, He had a reason. I knew that He could provide a ram. I knew that if He didn't, He was still good. I knew that this life, this business, this calling, all of it came from Him. He gives. He takes away. He restores. He gives back. He resurrects.

And He did.

25

Real Jesus

I had a guy reach out a few years ago, asking if I would meet for coffee. I had never met him. But I soon learned that we came from two entirely different worldviews. We became friends on Facebook, and when my world was opened to his world, it took me back a little.

His language is colorful, to say the least.

He's an equal opportunity offender.

The simplest summation of how he would describe himself would be a gay atheist witch.

He had asked to meet me, and as uncomfortable as the combination of all of those monikers might make me and many people in my tribe, I agreed to meet. In fact, I looked forward to it. I had no intention of arguing or debating with him. I just wanted to hear his story.

The day finally came, after many failed attempts to meet for coffee. We sat down, me with my black cup of coffee and him with a mango-peach smoothie. Straight away, I asked him to tell me his story.

At one point in his journey, he too had been a person of faith in Jesus. He attended church regularly, participated in all the events, even went on a few mission trips with his church. In his teen years, he began to wrestle with his sexual identity, and when he shared that with the leadership at his church, he was immediately ostracized and isolated. He no longer held to their worldview; therefore, he no longer mattered. The hurt he experienced turned him from a person of faith to a person who vehemently despised anything that bore the Christian label.

As I listened to him, I was reminded of the famous Gandhi quote in which he said, "I like your Christ. I do not like your Christians. Your Christians are so unlike your Christ."

I have had many conversations with my friend since that first conversation over a cup of coffee and a mango-peach smoothie. Time after time, he brings to me yet another instance where those who claim to follow Jesus represent Him in such a way that the true picture of Jesus can't been seen. We've made Jesus something that He isn't or never was.

I sat with my wife a few nights ago on our weekly date. Our conversation drifted to instances where she, too, as a Christian, had experienced deep, slow-to-heal wounds from some who would call themselves Christians.

"How is it possible that people who claim to know Jesus can act nothing like Him? Instead, they so naturally act the opposite of His character that we read about in the Bible."

I started to answer her question, to defend, to explain away. I started to give the benefit of the doubt. But I couldn't. All I could say was "I don't know, babe. I just don't know."

She's a pastor's wife who grew up as a pastor's kid. She had grown up her whole life around men and women of God. She had met a few who were the real deal, but there were some who talked a lot about Jesus, who sounded spiritual, but were a far cry from looking and acting like him.

A few weeks ago, a guy started attending our Sunday-morning gathering. He is generally the first person in the door, and while our worship team practices, he sits in a chair in the corner and reads his Bible and occasionally sings along. I soon learned after his first week of being with us that he was homeless and was trying to get back on his feet here in Chattanooga. He had moved here to be with his girlfriend, who ultimately dumped him, leaving him to feel rejected and alone, as if being homeless and camping on the doorsteps of a church wasn't depressing enough.

In typical RiverChurch fashion, our family members introduced themselves, got to know his story, and welcomed him into our family. One morning, he and I sat and had coffee together while Damon told me his story. His past was dark, and painful. He had lived through the agonizing loss of a young child, which created a domino effect of struggle for many years after. Eventually, he turned a corner and began walking a road to recovery and began making better choices for his life.

One such choice included going back to church. He went for a couple of weeks, but his tattoos and piercings made the church folks uncomfortable. At some point, someone in the church discovered some details of Damon's past and politely informed him one Sunday morning as he was about to come in that he could no longer attend that church. They were also uncomfortable with the piercings he had in his face, but he later learned they didn't want an "outlaw" in their church either.

He had almost given up on God, church, and anything remotely Christian. He was giving it all one more chance when he walked into a RiverChurch worship gathering.

"I was just glad to finally meet some Christians that really acted like Jesus."

The Sunday prior to our meeting, I gave an invitation for anyone who wanted to be baptized. As we continued to drink our coffee, Damon asked, "Can I be baptized?"

"Of course."

Two weeks later, at the end of our gathering, I invited Damon and the six other folks to come up front and to share with the congregation about their journey of faith and why they wanted to be baptized that day.

Kids and adults were getting baptized, so everyone's answers were so impacting. I walked over to Damon and asked him why he wanted to be baptized.

"I've wanted to follow Jesus. I've tried to follow Jesus. I've just been an outcast for so long, and I finally found a place and a group of people that would allow me to do it."

Tears began to fill the eyes of most of the people in the room. I waited a few seconds before I said anything.

I looked at Damon.

I looked at the crowded room.

"I'd just like to ask for any other outcast in the room to stand."

And like a wave of grace and acceptance, people began to stand up all over the room. Old and young alike. Kids stood. Teenagers stood. Men, women, everyone stood.

"Damon, look around. You're not alone."

Look, I've been one of those Christians who would have ostracized a gay atheist witch.

I've played the part of the man of God who didn't look or act very much like Jesus.

There was a day when I wouldn't want to worship with a tattooed, pierced outlaw.

I assumed that Jesus would only be in church around Christians, so that's where I wanted to hang out.

But my personal sin has also made me an outcast from what was good and holy, separated far from God. In reality, Jesus hung out with outcasts. He ate with them. He listened to them. He saw them not for what they had done but for what they could be. He showed people grace and mercy, and I needed that grace and mercy.

He served people, and that—that really is why Cadence exists.

We don't hide the fact very well that most anyone you meet at Cadence is a Christ follower. We often get the question, "Is this place a church?"

I like to think it's a place where Jesus, the real Jesus, would hang out.

I like to think He would sit with my gay atheist witch friend and have a cup of coffee with him.

I like to think that He would sit with the pastor's wife and listen to her, telling her, "I see you."

I like to think He would sit with the outcast and say, "Come follow Me."

I like to think, in fact it's my daily prayer, that when people come into Cadence, they see Jesus, not me or anyone else but the real Jesus behind the bar.

EPILOGUE

I seriously doubt that if Jesus were here on the earth today, He would be spending much time inside a church building. I'm not minimizing the importance or the need for the local church. I'm sure Jesus would join us for our gatherings each week. I hope He does now. But in my time at Cadence and pastoring RiverChurch, I can confidently say that the place I've seen Jesus the most often, day in and day out, is a little café on Seventh Street, downtown Chattanooga.

I would love to take credit for all the life-changing moments when we were able to impact someone's life for good. I have loved every opportunity we've had to offer someone a Pay It Forward, a warm meal, a blanket, a pair of shoes, a place to stay. I have found so much fulfillment in praying for people on the spot, having spiritual conversations over a hot cup of coffee, watching and listening to firsthand accounts of how lives have been changed through a small church and a little coffee shop that coexist in the same space daily. But every story, every last one of them, has been made possible only because of Jesus.

He has led us, He has called us, He has equipped us, and He has inspired us to love people who aren't like us, to see them as real people, to not just feed them but also eat with them. He has given us the grace to care for them when they were sick and to apply

Band-Aids and bandages when people came to us wounded. He's the one who told us to throw a lifeline to a person drowning in hopelessness and despair.

I guess what I'm saying is that Jesus called us to take the church to where the people are, rather than expect the people to come where the church is.

Every morning that we've opened our doors and every evening when we've closed them, He's been right there with us, behind the bar, challenging us every day to show people who might never have a chance to see a real picture of the real Jesus what He looks like.

A few weeks ago, as I was sitting with my Tuesday-morning group of guys, we went around the circle in typical fashion and checked in. Damon was talking about how amazing it had been to sleep in a bed for the first time in fifteen years. He was celebrating the fact that he had a place to come and sit for a few minutes with an iced chai before he went to his job at the vape shop around the corner. He looked at our group of guys and said, "I have family now. I have an outcast family, and it feels so good."

Do you know what made it possible for Damon to say that? Or should I say who made it possible? Jesus. He found Jesus, right where Jesus could be found. I'm not saying that Jesus would only be hanging out at Cadence Coffee Company. That's ridiculous. No, not at all. Jesus would be where people are—real people. Homeless people, rich people, divorced people, married people, anxious people, burned-out people, black people, white people, every-color-in-between people, gay people, straight people, addicted people; with these and so many other people would be where Jesus would be found.

He's where you go every day. He's at your office or at your school. He's in the park and in the store. He's walking on the sidewalk and at the restaurant. Here's the thing. He's right there with you, giving you the opportunities to team up with Him and to do exactly what He would do if you could see Him, if He were visibly present among us today. The question is, would you recognize Him?

Allow me to share one final story,

If she walked into a crowded room, you would be hard-pressed to miss her. She's tall, with long, thick blonde hair and a booming voice that would wake you from the deepest of sleep. Sarah was homeless, but she didn't spend a lot of time talking about that. She would tell you how good God had been to her. She bounced when she talked to you, side to side, like a basketball player, dribbling the ball up the court.

"He's taken care of me even when I didn't deserve it," she's said more than once to me.

One Sunday, she joined us for worship at RiverChurch, and man did she ever help me preach.

I'd make a point, and she would shout a hearty "Amen!" She would repeat the last word of my sentences with passion and conviction. She sang louder than anyone else in the room during worship, and I'm sure to some she might have been somewhat distracting, but I certainly wasn't going to tell her to be quiet.

I don't know all her story, but I do know she's had her fair share of dark days, sad days, and days of extreme need and loneliness.

At that time, we gave gift cards to first-time guests at RiverChurch for a free cup of coffee. Later that same week, she came bouncing into Cadence, waving her gift card in the air.

"What can I use this card for?" she asked.

"Anything you want!" I told her.

"Ooooooh, can I have one of them frozen drinks with some coffee and chocolate and caramel in it?"

"You sure can, Sarah!"

I made her drink, then slid it across the counter to her. She took a sip.

"Wooooooweeeee! That is *so* good!" She was loud and proud of that fancy drink.

She closed her eyes, squinting them as tightly as she could. Her fractured smile stretched from one side of her face to the other, and she just stood there fully embracing the moment.

"If my friends could see me now!" she shouted.

I could see her. I saw a grateful homeless woman enjoying a simple pleasure in life, but I saw something else too. I saw Jesus.

Just like I see him every day. Walking in with Nick and Gary, Gail, Kacey, Sam and Carl, Mary Lynn and Lynn, Marty and Lloyd, and every other person who walks through our door.

That's my view, every day, standing behind the bar.

As quickly as she had fluttered in, Sarah fluttered out, grabbing up her things, with a death grip on her chocolate and caramel blended coffee.

"God bless you, Pastor!"

And that, dear reader, is my prayer for you. God bless you. God bless you every day and everywhere you go to simply see Jesus wherever you see real people.

As for me, for my family, our RiverChurch family, we will be right here behind the bar, looking for more opportunities to be with Jesus, be like Jesus, and to do what Jesus does. Because …

There's more.

"For I was hungry and you gave me something to eat; I was thirsty and you gave me something to drink; I was a stranger and you took me in" (Matthew 25:35 CSB).

ACKNOWLEDGEMENTS

Kristia—When you said "yes" to me you never knew that our life together would look like it has. This life may not have been what you chose, but you have been right beside me every step of the way to watch God's story for our lives unfold. Early on in our marriage I told you that I never wanted you to walk behind me, or ahead of me, I wanted you to walk beside me. You have—faithfully. Thank you. I love you.

Makenzie—Your wide eyed wonder for the world inspires me to keep my eyes open to see more places where Jesus steps into our story. Thank you for reminding me to never stop looking. Thank you for loving Cadence, and coffee, and me enough to pour your life into seeing what happens next.

Madilynn—Your excitement to read every chapter of Behind The Bar as soon as it was written, often kept me committed to the process. You've been one of my biggest cheerleaders and a great hugger. Thank you for those raised eyebrows of anticipation. I live for them.

Josie—You embody the heart of compassion for those outside our circle. Your heart for justice and humanity and integrity challenges me to keep loving the unlovable. Thank you for offering your ideas of creativity not just to Behind the Bar but to my life in general.

Jayden—Thank you for walking right beside me. Your tender heart for the poor and the outcast as well as your friendliness to a stranger inspires me to always stay open for new friendships and new encounters with people. Thanks for always telling me that you think I'm cool. Being your role model is a high calling. I love you "captain." Let's go throw 100 pitches.

Arielle—You're too young to understand the significance that <u>Behind the Bar</u> carries as it pertains to your life. Had I never stepped behind the bar of Cadence, I might not have ever had the opportunity to be your dad. You truly are one of the greatest blessings to come from this story. Thank you for the morning snuggles, the sweet hugs & kisses, and "I love you daddy." Let me go get a fresh cup of coffee and let's snuggle on the couch and watch Bluey.

Mom & Dad—Here it is—that book you always encouraged me to write. You've always made it possible for me to go and do those things I felt like God would have me do. You've always helped make it happen when you could, and you've cheered for me along the way. I love you both. Thank you for pointing me toward Jesus as a small child, because of you I live with Him today.

Kimberly—Thank you for always making me feel like I could do anything I put my heart and soul into—for believing in me. I love you lil' sis.

Mom & Dad Utterback—Thank you for your unwavering love and support. From your faithful prayers for us each day to the many ways you show that you are "for us" you love well. Thanks for being part of our story.

Jacki, JonJon & Kiddos—Thanks for dusting off your barista skills "Wack"when we needed you and to both of you for being the best cheerleaders we know. Love you.

RiverChurch—To all our church family members past & present. Thank you for playing key roles in the stories included in this book. You have faithfully stepped behind the bar with me. Serving, giving, praying, crying, and loving just like Jesus does. Thank you for letting me lead you and to wear the hat of "pastorista."

Cadence Staff—(past & present) Thank you for contributing to the culture of coffee, community, and change. Without you there would be no story.

Trey—Thanks for being my "let's grab coffee" go to for more than a decade. From those first days at Starbucks to our Tuesday FaceTime Coffee Talks—you have proven to be my most loyal and best friend.

Jacob & Rachel—"Thank You" seems so small of a way to express my gratitude for the two of you. That cover though! You both are gold and I can't imagine walking this walk without you, both of you walking with us. Jacob thanks for your work on the cover. Rachel thank you for your open hands and readiness to help with any task—whether finding my keys, or spreadsheets with the most random data. I love you both—like family.

Lynn—Thank You for your immeasurable investment. God covers my rear, but you help in the process. There are no words to express my gratitude.

Ben—Thanks man for being a constant voice of encouragement. I am grateful for you and Pad Thai Tuesdays.

Tim, Sam, Brandon, Cameron, Michael, Harrison & Damon— Thanks for being my weekly place of guy time and inspiration. I love ya fellas.

Finleys, Holbrooks, & Russells—Thank you for being community for our family. For just being there, no matter what the need is. Burt & Chris—I've never had friends who would drop everything and come run "an intervention" like you. I've seen Jesus in the two of you standing in my kitchen helping me repair my cabinet doors and in so many other ways. I'll see you all Friday night.

Judy Hays—Thanks for proofing my first submission and your words of wisdom and guidance. You make the world better and brighter. I see Jesus in you.

Eleanor Sheeks—I never knew how much I would appreciate an English instructor's red pen. Thank you for continuing to encourage and challenge me to write more—I did.

Steve Grimes—Our lunches and conversations and your commitment to people like Rufus, as well as your desire to see Jesus everywhere you go, has encouraged me more than you will ever know. Thank you.

To the team of people at West Bow Press that made the dream of <u>Behind The Bar</u> a reality—thank you.

PGIL2023USA